Coming to America
A Journey Home

Hieu Tran
with Catherine Hackman

EBOOK   ISBN-13: 978-0-578-52683-6

PAPERBACK   ISBN: 978-0-578-52684-3

Dedication

For my three sons,
Ethan, Alex, and Evan.

Table of Contents

Chapter 1—A Daring Escape

Every person faces a defining question, an instant in which a choice is made that determines not only who that person is but also what he will become. While most people decide the answer to that question when they are adults, I chose when I was thirteen years old. My answer still resonates in my life today.

The night of the defining question was like any other night. It was October, 1987. A warm breeze blew through the gaps in the mud walls of our hut. Bugs, attracted by the dim light of the oil lamps, flew through glassless windows, easily finding their way to our skin, damp with oppressive humidity. This day had ended, like all of the others, with my sister, Chị, and me sitting on mats across a small fire from our mom. Our supper, as on most nights, was cassava, which is a root plant easy to grow in Vietnam. Mom would usually fix it the quick way by boiling it. On this night, however, she had strained it to get the juice out so she could make a pastry. After cooking it over the fire, she served us. Instead of using chopsticks, we broke off pieces with our fingers, like pizza dough.

"Má," I said to Mom through bites of the soft bread. "Please tell some stories."

I asked more out of habit than anything because the evening always brought anecdotes about the open market where she had spent the day selling vegetables.

"Today, there was a fancy lady in the market," Má leaned forward as she warmed to her story telling. "She had a fancy little dog in a purse which hung from her elbow. The dog looked like a little rat peeking out. . ."

She stopped mid-sentence when someone knocked on the flimsy covering which served as a door.

"Anh trai vào trong," Má called. It meant, "Brother, come on in."

The man who stepped across the threshold looked like any other man from our village, although he was probably a fisherman by trade.

"We leave now," he grunted.

Má slipped her hand under the mat where she had been sitting. As she extracted a plastic sack with a roll of yellowed tape, she motioned to Chị. My sister looked at the man, and then looked at Má.

"I don't want to go," she told them.

From the moment the man stepped into the

hut, Chị and I recognized him as a smuggler. He had the same nervous shift in his feet, the same urgent look in his eyes as the men who had led us on our two previous escape attempts. Chị knew what was coming. She didn't want to face it alone.

Má turned to me.

"You want to go?" she asked.

Right there, in a straw-roofed hut in the middle of a poverty-stricken village, I faced my defining question without realizing how important it was. I had experienced our previous bids for freedom as grand adventures. Since I had been young during our first tries, Má and Chị had shielded me from the arduous strain of an escape attempt. If I had known what was about to happen, I would have shrunk from the question by hiding behind Chị.

So in that moment, I made the biggest decision of my life without giving it any thought.

I said, "Yes."

I eagerly stripped off my shirt as my bare feet flew across the mat. While I held the plastic sack to my chest, Má walked around my body, taping the bag to my skin. She patted it carefully, perhaps thinking this would be the last time she would see her little boy. A couple of times she hesitated, adjusting the tape. She had planned to say, "Good-bye," to her

3

daughter; she hadn't prepared to lose her only son.

Anxiously, I kept my eyes focused on the guide. He seemed impatient to get moving. I thought this was the best game ever. I didn't want him to leave without me.

Má gave me a last hug, crying into my hair. I endured it as any thirteen-year-old boy would. I didn't comprehend that this was a one-way ticket. I didn't know anything, just that I wanted to get to someplace called America.

Chị gave Má's arm a gentle tug as the smuggler vanished into the night. If I didn't leave right away, he would be gone. I didn't look back as I followed his shadow-like figure into a rice paddy.

This is the house I lived in when I escaped Vietnam.

A bright moon lit our way to strange humping shadows clustered nearby. They stood to form the shapes of men and women who joined me in quietly sloshing after the guide.

A few hours later, toward the middle of the night, my legs started to ache from the struggle to keep up with the rest of the group. I was the youngest, and smallest, and nobody cared if I made it or not, least of all our guide. He already had Má's gold, and if I got lost, he knew she would assume that I had died like so many others who attempted this trip. Besides, she couldn't report him as a thief since what we were doing was illegal.

The guide was leading us through a mostly unoccupied stretch of land in Vietnam. A thin sliver of moon gave just enough light to reveal the shadows of the other men and women slogging quietly through the flooded rice fields. All around us was dark and quiet except for the sound of birds rising from the water at our approach. I briefly tried to imagine one of the shapes in front of me was Má, but I couldn't. Everyone in our group was short; Má was tall for a Vietnamese woman. Besides, if she was here, she would have been at my side, holding my hand, rubbing my back, urging me to press on. I didn't need her now anyway. I naïvely thought that I would see her again soon enough.

The guide must have given some sort of signal because everyone in front of me dropped as low as possible. I followed their actions. Water covered my thirteen-year-old body with only my head above the surface. As I crouched there on my hands and knees, I became aware of the sack stuck to my chest. Its tightness caused a bit of discomfort; the tape irritated my skin. However, its presence provided a measure of reassurance.

I knew the sack held important papers, but I didn't know what they were. Má had told me to give the packet to the people in charge when I came to something called a "refugee camp." Until then, it had to stay taped to my body. If the police caught us, I had to tear the papers to bits, eat them if necessary, so that the police could not discover the papers. Má told me if the police found the papers, they would kill me, then her and Chị.

A red headed cock crane flew over our heads; the white smear of the bird dipped and soared like a kite against the inky black night. The guide must have decided the movement he had detected in the dark was something harmless like a bird picking in the marsh for bugs because our group resumed its cautious movement through the water.

At the edge of the paddy, we started to descend. Although I couldn't see, I knew a village was at the bottom. The slush of the rice field gave way to tall grass. We pushed through it, by clasping our hands in front of us, then spreading them to make a way through. After a short distance, we stopped. Following the lead of the people around me, I sat in the jungle of grass. I didn't sense alarm on the part of the others, so I assumed we were waiting for something.

When we had huddled there for a long time, the adults became restless. Some of the group wandered a short distance to relieve themselves. Others took out food they had brought.

While I was running, I hadn't noticed how cold the night had become. Now, sitting there waiting, I started to shake. Putting my arms around my legs helped a little. I jumped when something touched my shoulder. One of the women in the group was so close her tunic sleeve brushed my hair when she moved.

"Con trai?" she whispered.

"Vâng," I breathed.

I was surprised that she said, "boy." Since none of the adults had acknowledged me, I had, up to then, believed myself invisible to all in our group except the guide.

An arm reached around my shoulder, gently pressing me to the warmth of the woman's side. She didn't say anything else. I must have slept because the next thing I knew, two shadows signaled the smuggler's return from the village with a young woman about my sister's age. I was disappointed that no young boys were with her.

As we started out, an entire flock of birds, Phu Quoc, judging from their oversized beaks and the white under feathers of their tails, rose from the rice field, screeching an alarm. This time, everyone started running. As I struggled to keep up, some rice strands tangled my feet, sending my entire body underwater. In just the brief time it took for me to right myself and start running again, the last adult had practically disappeared into the black. Police must be somewhere, in pursuit. The thought of someone jumping out of the dark to catch me gave me the burst of adrenaline I needed to catch up.

As the village disappeared behind us, the group gradually slowed to a walk. Someone in front of me stumbled, crying out. The guide shushed the person. I sensed everyone looking around fearfully. Two of the men took positions in back to survey the way we had come. They stayed there the rest of the journey, ready to signal at the least suspicious movement.

Eventually, our guide must have decided that we had eluded any pursuers because we stopped to rest in a field of soft grass. The guide gave each of us a ball of cooked rice. After we ate, we each took one sip of water from one of the water bags the guide had given the men to carry. Our rest was probably only ten minutes, but it gave us the strength to continue.

Finally, as the sky was turning from black to dark blue with the rising sun, our group arrived at the town of Bà Rịa-Vũng Tàu. We walked quietly around the outskirts until we came to the shore. The guide motioned to the men to follow him. They pulled a canoe from the bushes. After they dragged it to the water, we all got in. As the men paddled toward the channel, my toes pushed against the boat's splintery bottom. I was used to water, and I could swim, but being in that much water in a small, unstable craft was frightening. Other canoes emerged from the edges of the dark. I counted around 112 people.

Ahead, a small fishing boat waited for us. The front was shaped much like our canoe; the sides curved to a square back. A shelter, like a square hut, rose from the center. Fishing tackle, nets, buoys, and other accoutrements strewn about the deck gave it the appearance of a craft whose purpose was nothing more than catching fish.

When we boarded the boat, the women and children were placed in the cabin. That left the men, and me, on top of the shelter, exposed to the elements. One of the fishermen handed ropes to the other men and me.. I wasn't sure why I needed it, but I let it lie loosely over my legs. A brief survey told me that I was the only kid without an adult which was probably why I was placed on the roof. I felt mature, sitting with the other men.

At that point, during the other escape attempts, the authorities had come to escort us back to shore. I squinted hard in all directions. I didn't see anything but my guide and the others paddling the canoes to shore. The rough boards under me rubbed against my bare skin as the boat undulated with the motion of the water. A faint smell of fish wafted from the deck, and every once in a while, the wind carried the stronger odor of unwashed bodies to my nose. It looked like I would get farther into the game this time.

The men passed around a bowl. Each of us took a small ball of rice. After that, one of the fishermen gave us a sip of water. A gurgling roar accompanied by the nauseating smell of burning oil bellowed from inside the boat. As we lurched into motion, I grabbed the rope to keep from falling backward. The air cooled my skin, and the breeze on my face invigorated me. I laughed at the excitement of being underway.

After the first night on the boat came and went, I began to suspect something was wrong. The boat ride should have lasted only a few hours, not over a day. Worse, I was so nauseous from the movement of the small craft that I couldn't eat my share of rice or even force myself to sip water. None of the adults encouraged me. I was alone, and if I lived or died was none of their concern. I knew that if I did die, fishermen would throw my body into the ocean, and my mother and sister would never know what happened to me.

The plan was for us to go straight through to the refugee camp, but the second night into the trip, the boat ran out of oil. The fishermen hoisted the sail so the wind could move us. Mostly, we were just floating dead in the water. That made me sicker because the boat just rocked.

On the third night, there was a storm. I held onto the rope with my arms and legs, hoping the waves would not wash me into the sea. Each surge from the ocean filled my ears and nose with saltwater. I dry-heaved until I felt that my stomach would come up through my throat. Each bout of dry-heaving brought a wave of unbearable heat. When it was over, my body chilled until my teeth chattered. *If only the rocking would stop*, I thought. *I would be alright if the boat would just stop moving.* At that point, if I had lost my grip, I don't know if I would have even noticed.

I wanted Má. If Má was here, I thought, she would make the boat stop rocking. She would put her arms around me against the chills. Má would make it better.

This was when the enormity of what I was doing sank in. Má was my whole world up to this point, and I couldn't get to her, and she couldn't get to me.

I had heard her whisper to my sister about the dangers of the trip: sometimes people were intentionally pushed overboard, boats capsized, pirates took the escapees prisoner, people died from sickness and dehydration. Up to this point, the stories had only made the trip seem more exciting, but now, the danger was real, and it wasn't fun anymore; it wasn't a game.

There, on that rocking ship, with the waves threatening to push me overboard, with the nausea so strong I wanted to just give up, dehydrated and half-starved, I discovered something about myself: fierce determination. When I decided to do something, or I was put in a situation where I had no choice but to do it, I would find a way to do it.

I held on until my arms and legs seemed to be a part of the rope. There was nothing but me and the rope and the salt water and the terrible nausea. Once in a while, when the waves let up, I would feel for the plastic bag, check to make sure it hadn't floated into the ocean. Under my soaked shirt, the sack rested secure, a small sliver of hope that this terrible rocking motion and constant barrage of water would end eventually.

On the fourth night, there was a big ship out on the horizon, and the fishermen were able to use their lights to signal it. As it changed course, the men began to shift nervously. Some dropped to the deck and returned with oars or grappling hooks. Talk of fighting off pirates reached my ears. I was too sick to care.

When the ship was close enough, the men could see that it was a French cargo ship operated by an American company. Their fearful whispers turned to cheers of relief. As the ship pulled alongside us, I felt the boat tilt. People pushed to climb the rope ladder dropped by the sailors. I knew I had to climb too, but at that point, I was so sick, hungry, and tired. Physically, I couldn't do it. Mentally, I knew I had to move. If I didn't, I might be left behind. But I was too weak.

Then, I felt someone pick me up. The ropes fell away from my body as I rose to someone's shoulder. All I could do was lie there, folded over, and hope I wouldn't fall head-first into the ocean as the person climbed the long ladder to the deck of the ship. I don't remember what happened after we reached the top.

To this day, I don't know who picked me up. I like to think it was an angel who rescued me and then disappeared after I was safe.

Chapter 2—The Refuge

I opened my eyes to a carpeted room; I was on a bed with white sheets. For a boy used to sleeping on a dirt floor, it was like heaven. Everything was clean and white. And cold.

I had never experienced air-conditioning. It was strange.

Being in the big room alone was frightening. I could tell we were at sea by the rocking motion. I quickly felt for the papers. They were in the bed beside me. I moved the covers to see tell-tale black strips where the tape residue stuck to my now clean body. I didn't remember bathing or being bathed.

A man in uniform with very white skin came into the room with a tray. I ate a little. I went back to sleep, and when I woke up, the tray was gone. I slept for most of the rest of the trip, only waking a few times. It seemed like I slept for days. I don't remember going to a bathroom. I'm not sure if there was something in the room I used or if I went into an actual bathroom. I do remember that the first time I ate an apple was in that room. I thought it was the greatest thing ever.

I am not sure where the other passengers stayed during the trip. For a small boy to have an entire cabin to himself seemed extravagant and unrealistic. The answer to this unexpected circumstance was in the papers, the papers which remained beside me the entire voyage and were clutched in my hands when the white man in the uniform led me to the deck when the ship made port in Singapore.

As soon as the other refugees and I walked down the boat ramp, we got on a bus. Riding on a bus was a new experience for me. We went so fast. Besides Má's bike, the only vehicle I had ridden was a *xe lam*. A xe lam is like a rickshaw or a motorized tricycle with benches on both sides. It's very small and doesn't move very fast. Some would sit, and more would stand on the railing, hanging onto it. The fares didn't cost much, and the drivers packed as many people with packages on as possible to get the most money from each trip. On the bus, I had a whole seat to myself.

I shivered in the air-conditioning as I knelt on the hard seat with my face pressed against the glass. Everything was green. The color seemed surrealistic compared to what I was used to. The landscape of the rural area where I came from was hard-packed dirt mixed with clay. Occasionally we saw color when the rice undulated around us like tall grass, but it soon turned yellow-brown before the harvest. My eyes drank in the fresh beauty of the trees and plants. Everything seemed clean and unpolluted. Every once in a while, I would take a deep breath. Even the smell was clean.

The Singapore sky scrapers were just as amazing to me as the landscape. Up to this point, the tallest buildings I had ever seen were the three-story brick government buildings in the village where Má sold vegetables; here they rose around us, blocking the horizon. I pressed my cheek harder against the cold glass to view the sky above the tunnel of enormous structures.

The bus took us to a camp. There was a fence around it with vehicles coming in and out. Men in military-looking uniforms stood at the gate. It was a nice place, but it wasn't as nice as what we had driven through to get there. I was disappointed that the ground was dirt with no grass.

I clutched the plastic sack to my stomach as the other refugees jostled me in their excitement to get off the bus. When everyone was assembled, a relief worker told us to follow him. I pressed along with our group as we made our way to a large hut called the community building, where the relief workers served us a meal consisting of rice with fish and vegetables. After we finished eating, we stacked our bowls and chopsticks in an area to the side so the workers could wash them. I hid a little rice in my pocket in case they didn't have enough food for the next meal. As we walked around, I kept an eye out for a place I could eat in secret so that the others wouldn't steal what I had.

As we stood outside the next building, the relief workers gave each of us a small amount of money. I turned the coins in my palm, rubbing my fingers over the bumpy surfaces. I had never had my own money. The workers told us that the building was a store where we could buy candy or other small treats. I had a hard time believing it was all for me. Má rarely had any extras for candy; here, they just handed me money like magic.

I gripped the coins tightly as we made our way across the compound to the straw-roofed bamboo sleeping huts on stilts. The huts seemed to be about ten feet off the ground. We climbed the ladder of one to find it was another community room where the workers gave each of us a bamboo mat. I hid my coins in the center of the roll before carefully placing it to the side. The others might spend their money, but I would save mine in case they kicked me out of the camp. After I was sure my coins were safe, I couldn't wait for night to come; I had never slept that far off the ground.

There were other kids at the camp, most of them with families. Even though I had only been gone from my village for about a week, I felt like it had been a long time since I had played. I quickly made friends who ran among the huts with me. The plastic sack clutched in my fist flapped in the wind. The sheer pleasure of being clean with a full stomach in a safe place made all of us laugh at nothing.

An older boy made up a game of running and sliding under one of the huts. We each took a turn to see who could slide the furthest in the loose dirt. When my turn came, I ran extra hard, eager to show off how far my small body could skim across the open space. As I approached the area to slide, the older boy stuck out his foot, sending me sprawling. The plastic sack flew from my hand as I skidded toward the support pole of the hut.

When I righted myself, a little scratched, but mostly alright, I saw the older boy prying at the tape that sealed the precious bag of papers. Others crowded around him, anxious to find out what it held. A few yelled for me to get out of the way so they could take a turn at sliding.

My stomach knotted in panic. The older boy

wasn't much bigger than me, but I'd never been in a fight.

"Chào, đưa nó cho tôi," I commanded, trying to imitate Má's voice when she was angry.

They ignored me.

I pushed between two smaller boys to get closer to the sack. The older boy casually shoved me to the side. I held my ground, pushing against him as he held the sack away from me.

"Dừng lại!" a woman's voice commanded.

We all froze, obeying her sharp words.

I recognized the woman as someone I had seen in the community room. Every time I felt her eyes on me, she had given me a tentative smile. Earlier, she had been preoccupied with her two boys who looked to be around three and four years old. Now, she marched toward the older boy. Her children trailed after her, clinging to her loose pant legs and sucking on their fists.

Snatching the sack from the boy's grasp, she smacked him on the head. He ran off howling in the direction of one of the huts.

She held the packet toward me.

"Cảm ơn," I said gratefully, thanking her as I clutched it to my chest.

"What's your name?" she asked kindly.

"Hieu," I said.

"You can call me, 'Cô'," she responded. "Let's get your sleeping mat and move it next to mine."

After that, she and some of the other women watched over me as if they were my mothers. It gave me a degree of comfort to have someone to call to if something went wrong.

The next day, Cô took me to a busy hut near the community center.

"Give it to her," Cô told me, indicating a woman with pale skin sitting at a table just outside the entrance.

Shyly, I held out the sack. I felt a surge of panic as she slid a knife into the plastic to open it. 'What if I gave it to the wrong person?' I thought.

As the woman picked through the papers, I noticed how sharply the black hair falling to her shoulders contrasted with her white face. Casually, she handed the paperwork to the Vietnamese worker sitting next to her. He scanned it, then began speaking rapidly to the woman in a language I couldn't understand. He pointed to one area of the papers, then flipped to another and pointed again. She frowned.

"Go with her," the man said abruptly in

Vietnamese.

I took a step back to stand beside Cô, reluctant to go with this white woman.

"It's alright," Cô encouraged me. "I'll wait here."

"You can go with him," the man told her.

The white woman led us to another Vietnamese worker. He sat behind a table with a funny rounded box. The box had levers the man hit with his fingers. I liked the clicking sound and the little bell that dinged when he needed to push the rolling piece.

The man asked me a lot of questions. I didn't know the answer to most of them. When he asked about my Catholic faith, I looked at Cô, hoping for a signal as to how to answer. Má had said that not all areas of Vietnam allowed Mass; some officials held stricter views of its threat to communism than others. The people at this camp might not like Catholics; they might send me back if they knew. Cô, however, indicated that I didn't have to worry about telling the truth, so I answered every question.

The last topic was my father. We seemed to sit there forever while he asked me questions that I couldn't answer. I didn't know anything about my father except a brief story that Má told me once in a while. The topic of my father seemed to be even more significant to him than the fact that I was Catholic, however, because he motioned another man to come over. They discussed something assiduously, making sounds between them that I didn't recognize.

"Is he staying with you?" one of the men finally asked Cô. When she nodded, he wanted to know which hut was ours. She gestured to one close by.

"Bring him back tomorrow," the man said. "When you come, take him to the table over there." He indicated a table in a corner of the hut where a bored young man in uniform sat.

When we left the building, I ran behind one of the huts to relieve myself. Cô, who rounded the building a few seconds after I did, frowned when she saw what I was doing. She took me to central building with rows of stalls. Inside each stall were these things called toilets. She showed me how to use the toilet, including how and when to flush. I had never used toilet paper. Instead, my family used leaves, newspaper or anything else we could find. Toilet paper seemed too high-quality to use for that. The flush toilets were clean, and I was curious as to where the water, and everything, went. It was such a nice thing that I didn't have to smell the sewage, and there were stalls so that I could use the toilet privately. Back in Vietnam, a flimsy curtain around a hole in our yard was the only divider that kept my toilet practices from public view.

Using these toilets, and then the sinks, were the first time I encountered running water. I was curious about where the water was coming from and how it got there. How did it work for me to turn this thing on and there's the water? The water was better than what I had in Vietnam. Everything was better than what I had in Vietnam.

When Cô and I went back to the hut the next morning, the same young man in uniform sat behind the same table. Only this time, he didn't look bored.

"Hieu Tran?" he asked.

I nodded.

"You can come back later," he said to Cô.

This began a daily series of health exams, interviews, and screenings. Cô explained that they were making sure I was healthy and that I didn't carry any diseases. I just wanted them to get it over with as fast as possible so I could play with my friends.

One day, when I met the man at the table, he handed me an envelope. I recognized Má's handwriting scrawled across the outside.

As part of the arrangement, the smuggler had indicated to Má that he was taking me to a Singapore refugee camp, so Má wrote letters to me there. I was able to write back. Reflecting on this, I don't know how we were able to correspond since the Vietnamese government was suspicious of any mail from refugee camps, or America. It could be that since Má was a poor, insignificant peasant woman and the local authorities didn't know about her previous escape attempts, her mail just slipped in and out without any notice. Or, more likely, Má used black-market mail.

Each letter brought a wave of homesickness. I just wanted Má and Chị to be with me. I thought Má would somehow come up with the money for them to follow me, and each day, as more refugees arrived at the camp, I watched for them. Nights became harder after the letters started. Up to this point, I had always slept with the comfort of Má beside me and Chị just a few feet away. In the camp, alone, I started having nightmares about the storm on the ocean. Sometimes, when I woke up, Cô was there comforting me. Other times, I lay there shivering in the darkness, wanting Má to rub my back until the fear faded. I was at the camp for three and a half months. Má and Chị never got off a bus.

My stay was short considering that most people were there for years. People needed sponsors. People who didn't have sponsors were eventually sent to Thailand. In Thailand, sometimes the authorities sent them back to Vietnam. I didn't have a sponsor; I had something better: the pack of papers. In addition to moving me through more quickly, the information in those papers provided me with a ticket to anyplace in the world.

No one at the camp told me any of this. The relief workers simply asked me where I wanted to go. Right away, I said, "America." It was the place I had dreamed about my entire young life. It was the only place I knew.

Chapter 3—Leaving

On the night before I left, the camp barber cut my hair which had always been a bit long. The next morning, Cô helped me dress in a pair of slacks, almost like khakis, with a long-sleeved, button-down shirt with a collar. After wrestling my first pair of real shoes onto my feet, she tied the laces, then helped her children maneuver the ladder. She frowned as I descended. I had left the socks on, but the shoes were thrown on the sleeping mat. They were hard; I didn't like them. She firmly told me to keep them on as she laced them a second time. The coins I had hidden in my socks had slipped under my feet by this time, making the shoes that much more uncomfortable.

After breakfast, Cô hugged me like Má had done on the night I left. This time, I didn't squirm away. I didn't know what was going to happen, just that I was going to America.

While I was on the plane, I remember being scared. The first time I felt the plane taxi and go up was amazing. I was mesmerized by how the plane could fly. I knew I had one stop. Instead of a plastic sack taped to my body, I had a name pinned across my chest which had to stay there no matter what. The plane stopped somewhere a few hours after take-off. As soon as I got into the terminal, someone holding a sign with my name on it grabbed me and put me on the next plane.

The other people on the flights were of mixed nationalities, but I was the only refugee passenger. On the plane, no one communicated with me. When the stewardess set a tray of food in front of me, I was relieved. I could save the rice I had stuffed in my pocket to eat when I got to America.

As the flight became longer and longer, I thought about some strange things associated with the camp at Singapore. I had heard adults talking while we were eating. Please change to "Most of them said an escape had cost them ten thousand to thirty thousand American dollars per person; it had to be paid in gold. Altogether, Má, Chị, and I had made the equivalent of seven escape attempts. Hearing that price made me wonder. Má couldn't even afford a new bicycle to take her vegetables to market. How could she pay the equivalent of seventy thousand American dollars for these attempts? The adults at the camp must have been mistaken, or they exaggerated like most adults do when complaining about money.

Also, the workers at the camp had been really

interested in my father. I couldn't figure out why. Má hadn't spoken of him much, and I hadn't been curious enough to ask. Now, as the plane carried me further and further away from Má, I wished she was there to tell me more. But even if she was there, I knew she might not tell me what I wanted to know. Má, who was known to her friends and relatives as Lua Tran, was a fierce secret keeper. I found out much later in life that she had to be in order for us to survive.

Even though my birth certificate says I was born in July, Má says my real birthday is April of 1974; my sister Loan was four years old when I was born. Since she was older than me, I called her Chị out of respect. On the few occasions that I asked her about our dad, she told me that she didn't remember much about him. I didn't remember anything. He was a ghost that should have been with us, but wasn't.

Má almost never talked about him except to say he was a very mild-mannered, soft-spoken guy. Of the two of them, Má was the talker. People said dad was shorter. That is all I knew about my father for a very long time. He was the biggest secret in my life. Má hadn't told me that he was a dangerous secret that could have killed all of us if it were discovered. He remained a stranger shrouded in mystery until well into my adult life.

Sending her only son on such a risky venture was not an easy decision for Má, but escape was of the utmost importance to her. After the Vietnam War ended, she knew that if we were ever going to get out of hardship, we had to get out of Vietnam. She had big dreams for our path of life.

We heard a lot about America being the land of opportunities, that all you had to do was work hard, and you would get what you wanted. Even if you didn't have money, you could borrow money to go to school. Our vision of America was like heaven: everything was perfect; everything was so much better than what we had in Vietnam. We could have electricity, we could buy a house, and we could buy cars: a car for my Má, a car for Chị, and a car for me, instead of one bicycle for the whole family. That's what we thought of America. That dream was very enticing; something Má wanted to make a reality: she desperately wanted to take Chị and me to America.

Má's accumulation of enough gold for seven attempts was even more unbelievable considering how difficult surviving without a husband was for a Vietnamese woman. Before our first escape attempt, Má owned land. The harvests from that land brought barely enough to support us at poverty level; selling the land would not have brought enough to pay for even one of us to escape. How she owned this land without the communists confiscating it was another great mystery.

No one encountering Má would have suspected that she had a small fortune. To all appearances, she was a typical Vietnamese widow. She worked very hard to grow rice and vegetables. After harvesting, she loaded the produce on the back of her bicycle so she could take it to the market where she sold it to the public. Although she never had a formal education, she was a very shrewd businesswoman. Even with all her dedication, we didn't have much. Our straw-roofed shack had a mud floor. It was actually a dirt floor, but the roof leaked, so when it rained outside, it rained inside, turning the floor to a slimy muck. The walls were mud with gaps. When it was windy outside, it was windy inside. We didn't have electricity, so we used oil lamps for light. At the time, the more well-off people would buy a car battery so they had electricity. When Má was a land owner, before our first escape attempt, it stands to reason that we would have had a car battery, too. We didn't.

There were other things we didn't have. We didn't have running water. No plumbing. The bathroom was a hole we dug in the back yard. Má erected a bamboo frame around the hole with leaves or a cloth covering it to give some privacy. The worst part was the smell. The smell of that hole reached all the way to the house, attracting flies along with other unsavory insects. When the contents of the hole neared the top, we would fill the pit with dirt after digging another one.

Our water supply came from our well just a few feet from the house. I don't recall how we got our own well; it was just always there. Of course, it wasn't an electric well. A post stood on either side of the hole with a wheel and axle hung between them. A bucket dangled from a rope on the wheel. We would send the bucket down, then reel it up before pouring that water into a different bucket to carry it to the container next to the wall. If we were thirsty, we dipped water out of that bin to drink. Chị and I kept the container full; we also brought extra water for Má when she needed it.

In spite of our poverty, Má made sure we had basic necessities. My long hair was the social norm at the time, but it still needed to be trimmed. There was a barber shop where Má was able to pay to get my hair cut, but the majority of time, she clipped it herself. She and Chị always had long hair, so I was the only one who needed a trim. She bought our clothes. I don't know how or where. I wore pants or shorts with a shirt. I went barefoot, except when I went to church or school; then, I wore slippers. As for her and Chị, they wore long, loose pants and long, loose shirts. Each of them also wore a nón lá, which is a large, cone-shaped, bamboo hat. Má valued light skin, so she always made sure that she and Chị had clothes that blocked the sun. We all had toothbrushes and toothpaste. She taught us to brush our teeth after washing our faces as our morning routine. We would bathe, but not very often, usually in the rain.

Although Má was a fierce secret keeper and businesswoman, she was not an unfeeling person. Often when I was younger, she would come up to rub my leg or my shoulder to show motherly affection. At times when the weather was especially hot, she would give me some air by waving her hand-held fan. All of her actions showed a deep love for Chị and me.

Chị helped a lot with the field work as well as with caring for the chickens and pigs. I didn't do much because I was young and because I was a boy. When I was with Má, I followed her around like most little kids do. When I went with her to the market, I rode on the handle bars of her bike. Even though I didn't have regular chores, I absorbed one of life's key lessons from her: *You always have to work for what you have.*

Someone had to be at the hut at all times, or people would steal our cooking utensils and chickens. As far as I knew, that was all we had of value, and we needed what we had. We had no way to lock up when we left. Chị quit school after the fifth grade so she could stay home to watch the house. When she quit school, the resources that had gone toward her education went to mine. Society at the time thought the girl didn't really need to be educated because she would get married and take care of a family.

This brings up another mystery about money. Sending a kid to school was expensive. Parents had to pay school fees in addition to purchasing a uniform. Each kid had to be in uniform; kids couldn't just wear anything they wanted. The school uniform was very formal: plaid shorts, a blue or white collar shirt with a neckerchief, and flip flops. I had two uniforms. Whatever unknown sacrifices Má had to make to send me to school were well worth it for her; Má valued education. For her, education meant getting a better job, plus status with the community.

The school system in Vietnam was a little bit different from the American way of educating. The children stayed in the classrooms, and the teachers switched rooms, unlike in America where every period the students have to move to different classrooms and different teachers. Also, the children didn't go to school all day. Either they went in the morning and got out at noon, or they went at one o'clock and got out at four o'clock. Kids went to either but not both. Before she quit, Chị went to morning school. I went in the afternoon so there was always someone to watch the house. School was six days a week with Sundays off.

When I wasn't in school, my time was spent doing the typical things that boys do. I went to my friends' huts to play, or they came to my hut. There were mountains nearby, so we would go up to the mountains to climb trees, catch crickets, and so forth. Of course, we didn't have the technology that kids have today. Everything we did involved manual labor. If we wanted a toy, we had to make it.

One of the most fun things my friends and I did, and the thing that got me into the most trouble, was making kites. At school we learned how to make kites out of newspaper, or out of school notebook paper. Bamboo provided the supports. Since didn't have glue, we smashed cooked rice on two pieces of paper to stick them together. To fly the kites, we would go out to the streets or into rice paddies that had already been harvested. The problem was, school notebook paper was expensive, and Má had to buy the notebooks, so tearing the paper up was a waste of resources. Má always got really upset at me. She would beat my hands and spank my butt. That did not stop me from making the kites, however, so her punishment couldn't have been too harsh.

The bump of the plane's wheels lowering accompanied by the queasy feeling of my stomach momentarily rising and falling told me that the plane was landing. I didn't know it at the time, but I was at O'Hare airport in Chicago, Illinois. What I did know was that I had reached this place that Má had talked about for as long as I could remember. A place where I could get as much rice and paper to make as many kites as I wanted. I was in the United States of America.

Chapter 4—The Mythical Land: America

My first thought as I looked around the airport was that it was huge. Planes were everywhere. There were all kinds of big, white people pulling suitcases, carrying briefcases, balancing cups of coffee while holding a magazine. All I had was my clothes. I didn't have a bag or anything. I had never been around so many white people. I immediately went into culture shock.

As I entered the terminal, a Vietnamese man walked toward me with a big grin.

"Xin chào, Hieu," he said.

Hearing the Vietnamese language helped me to relax.

He explained that he was an interpreter for Tha Huong, which was a group home for refugee children, also known as a residential facility. As he spoke, he held out a cumbersome, tunic-looking thing by the shoulders.

"Put this on," he said.

I frowned at him. That bulky piece of clothing would suffocate me in the heat. That's when I noticed that many people walking past had on similar, large coverings. Má had talked about how strange the Americans she had met during the war had been.

Maybe this was one of their strange customs. I didn't want to offend the man, so I put my arms into the tight sleeves, which pulled my shirt sleeves up to my elbows. The slick inner material felt good against my skin. I followed the man through the airport; right before we went outdoors, he paused to zip the covering.

When we stepped outside, the cold took my breath away. For me, seventy-five degrees was cold, and now I was thrust into what seemed like an arctic chill for the first time ever.

The ground was covered in white shining mounds.

"What's this white stuff?" I thought. I bent to touch it. It was cold.

"Snow," the interpreter said with a grin.

I had seen cars before, but in Vietnam there were fifty bicycles to one car. In Chicago, there were cars everywhere. It seemed like everybody had a car. I remember thinking that maybe I could get a car someday.

While the interpreter drove, he explained that there were refugee camps all over the world. And at these refugee camps, there were non-profit organizations that would accept kids and families, like me. The camp where I had stayed was a mission outreach of the Catholic church. Department of Children and Family Services (DCFS)-Sponsored Catholic Social Services had brought me to America, and now we were going to this place called *Tha Huong* in a city called Peoria. The primary goal at Tha Huong was to give unaccompanied refugee children a safe environment to land in before they moved on to American foster families. Unlike orphanages where the goal was to find people to adopt the children, the kids at Tha Huong were not adoptable because we still had parents, and technically, our mothers and/or fathers still had parental rights. So we would always be in the foster system until we reached age eighteen and could graduate out. He also told me about the upcoming interviews and medical exams and not to be afraid.

Later, the same man interpreted as my case worker asked questions about my social history so people would know what kind of family I had in Vietnam, how I arrived in the United States, and whether I had experienced significant trauma along the way. I also went through a series of medical exams. Since I had gone through a similar process in Singapore, I wasn't as afraid as I otherwise might have been. I arrived in the United States in February of 1988. The minimum stay at Tha Huong was six months. I was there for only six months.

Most of the kids who arrived at Tha Huong didn't know English. The few who were pretty good in English were usually from wealthy families in Vietnam and, therefore, were better educated. The group home consisted mainly of boys, about ten at a time. Through the years, the most girls who were there at any one time was seven to eight. The girls all stayed in one room, and the boys were housed mostly in one big dorm room with bunk beds. Although the home was made up predominantly of Vietnamese, there were a few Cambodians and one boy from Thailand.

Tha Huong had Vietnamese child care workers. There were three different shifts, so there was twenty-four hour staffing of this residential facility. If I needed something, I went to see one of these workers. Since the goal was to help us assimilate into the American culture, they taught us the basic things like how to use a toilet. Some kids did not even know how to do that. How to use a tissue to blow our noses was very important—at least to one cleaning lady. She would find stuff, in the shower, in the garbage cans, wherever. Our laundry situation was unique. One boy brought back a pair of pajamas from his potential foster mom. The workers said he couldn't put them in the laundry because he probably wouldn't get them back to wear the next time. The workers did all of the laundry together, and we grabbed whatever would fit. We had clothes, but we didn't own them.[1]

I learned one way the Asian culture is different from the American culture the first time I watched television. One of my friends told me to come into the main area to see a show called *Tom and Jerry*. I flopped on the floor in front of the couch where a couple of the other boys were wrapped up together laughing at the cartoon cat and mouse antics. In the Asian culture, it was not uncommon to see guys with their arms around each other walking down the street or laying on the couch wrapped up together; however, doing those things was not acceptable behavior in America at that time. When one of the workers saw them, she told them to sit on opposite ends of the couch while explaining why it was unacceptable to do that in the United States.

The meals introduced us to American food, but all we wanted was ramen noodles. We called them just *noodles*. The American workers always enjoyed our authentic Vietnamese cooking, so often, the cooks would allow us to make the Vietnamese food, which is how I first encountered a refrigerator.

The blast of cold accompanied by the light fascinated me. I opened and closed the door fast to see if the light stayed on all the time. Finally, one of the workers told me firmly to stop and shooed me away from my newfound toy.

I was not at Tha Huong for the "Tet," Vietnamese New Year, but Tha Huong would celebrate it with the dragon dance and the whole thing. The children also had several different religions. One of the rules was that the group home had to accommodate the boys' religion as much as possible. Some of the kids were Buddhists, so they would be able to go to the Buddhist temple once or twice a year or every several months. The staff had to drive them to Chicago for them to attend. Some of the other boys and I were Catholic, so that made it easier because Tha Huong was run by Catholic Social Services. Every week we were able to go to Mass. There were a handful that were Protestant, so they were able to go to church easily, also.[2]

I received four letters from Má which had been forwarded from the refugee camp in Singapore. At this point, I became extremely homesick for her and Chị. As I settled in here, I missed the comfort of having them close to me, of being able to rely on them to help me, of having them do things for me.

Since I was the youngest, and a boy, they had lavished their love and attention on me. I don't remember what I wrote, but I sent letters to Má. At about this time, Tha Huong helped me file Affidavit of Relationship papers so that Má and Chị could come to the United States. If I didn't receive a letter from Bangkok, Thailand, within one year, an adult was supposed to help me contact the Refugee Resettlement Office in Peoria, Illinois.[3]

We had a school on campus, Tha Huong School; its purpose was to help us to learn enough English so that we could transition into American public school. Every day I went to the classroom where the instructors tried to teach the culture and the language. I was only in the school for a few hours. Then, I went back to the group home where I spoke Vietnamese to my friends. For that reason, I didn't learn much English while I was there.

In order for me to be deemed ready to leave the place, I had to know the culture, learn a little English, and agree to the home they found for me. All three had to come together for me to be able to actually leave.[4] At this point, though, I liked where I was. I had friends, I had plenty of food, and I had a clean place to sleep. Living with a foster family was the farthest thing from my mind.

A picture of me after I arrived in America.

Chapter 5—A Couple Taking in a Refugee

At around the time of my Vietnamese family's first escape attempt, a man and woman 8,680 miles away saw a commercial on television about adopting Vietnamese refugee children. Although they had two daughters still living at home, the opportunity to foster one of these children caught their attention.

The next time the commercial came on, the woman turned to her husband.

"Ernie," she said. "We've never had a boy."

Without much hesitation, he responded. "Well, Sheryl, I think it would be a good idea to take in one of those kids."

Right away, Sheryl plucked the phone from the wall to dial the number.

"DCFS," a woman's flat voice answered.

"Oh, I'm sorry," Sheryl said. "I must've dialed the wrong number."

"Who are you trying to reach?" the woman on the other end huffed.

"We want to adopt one of those Vietnamese orphans," Sheryl explained.

The woman's voice changed.

"You have the right number," she said with a

45

touch of excitement. "Just to explain: they are not orphans, they are refugee children who don't have a parent or family member with them. Different organizations sponsor the children, but DCFS actually finds the homes."

The woman went on to explain that whenever someone called about taking in a refugee, DCFS would do the home study and the training to see if the family provided a viable home. In addition, DCFS would look to see if other Vietnamese kids were nearby that so that the kids could connect with someone familiar to them culturally. The family had to be willing to help the kids visit other Vietnamese kids to help with the transition. That was part of the planning as to who would go to which home.

Once a home was approved, a child would visit that home. If that went well, there would be one or two more visits—one might be overnight, just to see if the child could connect with this family. If the family said, "No, I don't want that child," or if the child said, "No, I don't want this family," DCFS started looking into other placements. It wasn't like "Here's a warm home, let's put 'em there."

After the and a half-long process of fingerprints, background checks, and foster care training, Sheryl and Ernie Layton were able to bring home their first boy, a fifth or sixth grader. He didn't know his birthdate. An American soldier found him in a ditch by his mom after she had died. His name was Giang. Two more Vietnamese refugees, both boys, came while the first one was still with the Laytons. These boys were older. They were only with the Laytons for two years before they decided they wanted to live someplace else. After they left, Sheryl and Ernie asked their daughters what they would think if they got another boy.

The girls, grown adults by now, had both moved out, so they said, "Do what you want."

Giang, still living at home, had graduated high school; he worked, and wasn't there much, so he didn't care.

The Laytons once again applied to take in one of the refugees. At the same time, I was near the end of my stay at Tha Huong.

During my time in Peoria, I was assigned to a case worker. Her name was Tina. I thought she was beautiful. She had been working with me for a couple of months when she told me that she wanted to take me to meet some people who might be my new family. I wasn't sure I wanted a new family. I didn't understand why I couldn't just stay there. The interpreter echoed Tina's reassuring tone as she translated that if I didn't like the people, I didn't have to stay with them. She asked me to try. Tina's face showed how much she cared about me. I said one of the few English words I knew, "Okay."

The drive from Tha Huong to the Laytons took an hour each way. Tina was the one who drove me. She didn't speak Vietnamese. I could only say a few words to her in English. The absence of an interpreter made the trip seem longer than it actually was.

The Laytons lived in Havana, a small town on the Illinois River. Population 3,200 people and shrinking. No other ethnic group but me. That's Havana.

Tina parked in the drive of a square house with wooden shingles. A tall woman with brown hair opened the door.

"Come on in," she said in a voice full of welcome.

The air in the house surrounded me with cold as I stepped out of the hot late-July sun. I still wasn't used to homes being a constant temperature of about seventy-five degrees, no matter what the temperature outside was.

"Ernie, they're here," the woman shouted. She smiled at me. "I'm Sheryl."

I nodded, not sure if I should speak.

A man, about a head smaller than Sheryl held out his hand as he entered the room.

"I'm Ernie," he said. His t-shirt and jeans smelled of oil and dust. Letters over the brim of his hat spelled "ADM." He said something to Tina that I didn't understand. I did understand the words "shower" and "work."

"Hungry?" Sheryl asked.

I was always hungry, even when I was full.

She led us into the kitchen where she opened a large refrigerator. I was amazed at the shelves and shelves of food.

She and Tina talked to each other as she set cookies and milk in front of me. I thought the soft, sweet cookies had to be the best thing I had ever tasted. I snuck two into my pocket in case Tina left me here, and these people didn't give me anything else to eat.

After I finished, Sheryl showed Tina and me the house. It was huge, and very clean.

Finally, Sheryl knocked on a door at the end of a hall. After someone inside yelled something, she led us into a huge room. A man got up from where he was sitting on a bed, fiddling with some kind of box-looking thing.

This is when I got excited. He was Vietnamese like me. I started talking to him, asking him his name and where he was from in Vietnam. He looked at me blankly while he shook his head. I slumped inside when I realized that he didn't understand me.

"Giang," Sheryl said, gesturing to him.

He held out his hand in the American gesture of a handshake. I let him move my hand up and down.

Sheryl stood beside a bed opposite the one where Giang had been sitting.

"Hieu," she said, slapping the blue comforter.

I understood that I would sleep in this room with Giang. I hadn't seen anyone else so far. I wondered if the other kids slept on the floor.

Ernie came in while we were standing there. Now, he smelled like soap, and his short brown hair was slightly damp.

He said something I didn't understand, but it ended with "Hieu," so I nodded.

On the drive back to Tha Huong, I kept thinking, "This is a huge, clean house. They seem like nice people. They've got food. They've got a room for me, with my own bed. It seems like it's nice."

The second time Tina took me to visit, I stayed for one day. When we got back to Tha Huong, a translator helped me discuss living with the Laytons. I told Tina that I was ready to leave Tha Huong, but that I was sad to leave my friends. I also told her that I was afraid.

The third time Tina dropped me off, she cried. Then, I knew I was staying forever. Even though we had talked about it, I didn't truly comprehend that I was staying there permanently until she left.[1]

Sheryl and Ernie took me out to eat for the first time a few days after I started living with them.

"Hieu, we're leaving," Sheryl told me.

As she opened the door, I saw Ernie starting the car.

Instead of going with her, I ran to my room. It was supper time. Maybe they were going to dump me off somewhere because they ran out of food. Quickly, I stuffed the bread and apple hidden under my bed into my pockets.

"Hieu," Ernie said, appearing at the door. "Go." Evidently, he didn't think I understood.

Reluctantly, I climbed into the car.

I listened to the sound of Sheryl and Ernie's voices as we drove into town. We stopped in front of a large building with a lot of cars in the parking lot.

Maybe they were going to sell me to a different family. When Sheryl opened her door, the smell of grease wafted into the car. My stomach grumbled, but I sat in the car, hoping they would change their minds.

"Hieu, come on," Ernie said. His pleasant voice reassured me that maybe they weren't going to get rid of me.

The back of my legs stuck to the plastic seat of the car as I scooted toward the door. I rubbed them to get the stinging sensation out as we stepped into a warm room full of people sitting at rectangular, wooden tables. Cigarette smoke made the air slightly cloudy even though only the people in one corner smoked. A large square partition took up the center of the room. Inside the partition, a woman served bottles and glasses of liquid to the people on the stools surrounding it.

"Three, non-smoking?" A woman with her hair in a pony-tail asked as she led us to the far side of the room.

My bare skin made squeaking noises as I slid across the slick vinyl of the booth seat. The woman jabbered something, scribbling on a small tablet when Ernie said something back. She placed a large two-page book with pictures of food and writing on it in front of each of us and left.

I got on my knees so I could peer over the back of the seat. So many people speaking so fast. Not one of them had dark skin like me. I felt overwhelmed.

"Hieu," Sheryl said sharply, frowning.

I wasn't sure what I did wrong, but I sat facing her with my hands in my lap.

The pony-tail woman returned with a tray balanced on her hand. She set a glass of soda in front of me before she started writing on the tablet again. Sheryl gestured at the pictures as she talked to the woman.

Then, we just sat there. By this time, I had figured out that this was a place to eat. Although I had never eaten at a restaurant, once or twice Má had been able to afford phở , a noodle soup sold at stands in the market. A serving hadn't amounted to much, so I didn't expect to fill my stomach here. I was glad I brought extra food along.

When the waitress came back the next time, a man followed her. Both had trays heaped with food. She set a plate in front of me with a large hamburger, piles of French fries, and some kind of green shredded vegetable in a white sauce.

I looked around the table. Ernie and Sheryl

each had a plate loaded with food, so the meal must be for me. I couldn't believe Ernie and Sheryl could afford to pay for so much food at once, served to us at a table in a building. I ate until I felt sick. The food was so good, and I didn't want to be ungrateful by wasting it. While I was still trying to stuff fries into my mouth, the waitress scooped my leftovers into a brown sack. When we got home, Sheryl put it in the refrigerator while explaining that I could eat it for lunch the next day.

The week after I moved in with the Laytons, I went to school. That was when life got tough. I enrolled in the seventh grade in September of 1988, at the local junior high.

My first class of the day was science. The teacher looked more like a bear than a man. Compared to my small body, he was enormous. His name was Butch Howarth, but I called him Mr. Howuhd. He placed me in a seat in the front row in a corner.

The other kids started whispering. The low, fast sound made me dizzy, so I stopped trying to pick out words I knew. Then, a skinny kid with light brown skin and really short hair said, "Vietmanese," really loud. The other kids laughed.

I had noticed him right away because of his

darker skin; he wasn't as dark as me, but he was less white than the others.

I said, "Hello."

That sent the light brown kid into peels of loud laughter. The others joined in. I laughed, too. Maybe, "Hello" wasn't what I was supposed to say, or maybe Americans just laughed for no reason.

The class was talking about outer space. I learned the English word "planet" and the word "moon." I couldn't understand anything else that happened, but I was pleased with my two new words.[2]

After that, I followed the kids to my next class. This teacher, also a man, was arguably larger than the first one. He had bushy brown hair surrounding a face with a large mustache over his upper lip. When he saw me, he broke into a huge smile.

His voice boomed something too fast for me to understand.

By this time the other kids had taken their seats. They all chittered excitedly.

"Mr. Schroeder," the big man said, thumping his chest with his palm.

"Mr. Shredder," I mimicked. From the way he and the kids laughed, I knew I didn't get it quite right. I smiled along, assuming they were laughing with me, not at me.

He handed me a heavy, hard-cover book before leading me to a seat in the middle of the room.

The light brown boy opened my book to a page with strings of symbols I recognized as the letters of the alphabet. He pointed, saying something. I put my finger where he put his. He nodded, seeming pleased that he had somehow communicated with me.

The teacher started talking in the rhythmic tone of storytelling. After a few minutes, he stopped. The kids put their hands up. He pointed to one who took up the cadence. I figured out that they were reading from the book, but I couldn't understand what they were saying. The pictures helped me know the story was about people who seemed to be a family. I wasn't sure how each kid in the class knew when to stop reading, but one after another the students took up the rhythm of the words. When one stumbled, the teacher's booming voice softened as he pronounced the sounds slightly differently.

Once in a while, the teacher would say something which prompted the class to burst into laughter. I laughed, too, even though I didn't know why. I liked being a part of the group. When the reading stopped, the teacher gave each of us a white piece of paper smudged with purple letters; it smelled faintly of chemicals. The rest of the kids put the paper into a folder, so I did, too. This was great! The teacher was giving us free paper. I could make as many kites as I wanted after school.[3]

For the rest of the day, the teachers would show me pictures and talk to me, but I had no idea what they were saying. I could tell they were trying hard. Every teacher gave me kite paper which I stowed away in my folder.

At lunch, the light brown boy pulled me into the line with him. He showed me how to get the tray, pick out silverware, and push along the shelf so the lunch ladies could load on food. I couldn't believe it; they were just giving me food. I decided I wouldn't need the biscuits I had hidden in my pockets.

I followed the light brown boy to a table where a tall, dark-haired kid was stuffing his face with mashed potatoes.

The light brown kid pointed to himself, "David."

"David," I repeated slowly. For some reason, that sent him into uncontrollable laughter.

When he could talk again, he pointed at the kid sitting at the table, "Jeff."

The kid looked up briefly before he resumed shoveling food into his mouth.

From that moment on, we three were inseparable.[4]

When I got home from school, I showed Sheryl the folder with the treasure trove of papers. She grabbed a pencil from a drawer, indicating for me to sit at the table. One by one, she took out each paper. I frowned when I realized that I wasn't going to be making kites. She guided my hand to make marks on the paper with the pencil. I had no idea what we were doing. At long last, all of the papers were back in the folder. Wisely, she put the folder away. My plans to look through the cabinets for rice crumbled.

Sheryl started putting dishes on the table, and Ernie took his customary seat. While we were eating dinner, a boy from my class called and wanted to talk to me. Sheryl handed me the phone.

I said, "Hello," then handed the phone right back to her because I couldn't carry a conversation.

At that point, I realized that not being able to communicate presented a real problem.

Up until then everything was a new adventure, and I'd had other Vietnamese to talk to. When I was in Singapore, there were other

Vietnamese. Peoria also had other Vietnamese. Having them filled the hole leaving Má had made in my life. Plus, I wrote to her all the way up to Peoria. She got the letters, and she wrote back. Once I got to Havana, I didn't get any more letters. Now that I was in a safe place, the anger, sadness, and loneliness, which the excitement of the trip had shadowed, came rushing out. I laid in my own bed that night with a full stomach, clean clothes, and my own television; I had everything I had dreamed of having, yet I felt small and alone.

That's the first time I wished I hadn't left. I thought about how Má struggled to raise us. As much as she worked, and she worked hard, we never had the hope of having anything significant. I saw others that had some things that I didn't, but I knew I could always depend on Má for comfort and care. And then when I came over here, I didn't have anybody to lean on for support, no family, and no one who spoke the same language I did. With all of my being, I wished I could go back to Má. I needed Má so badly right then, to hug me, to tell me everything would be alright.

I started to blame Má. Why did she let me go? I blamed myself. Maybe I didn't do my chores enough, and she wanted to get rid of the extra burden.

Maybe if I promised to help more, she would let me go back. I was so angry with her. She could have told me that I needed to do more instead of just sending me away. I decided to write to her in the morning to see what I had to do for her to take me back.

I wrote the letter, tore it up, and wrote it again. Except to eat, I stayed in my room the entire weekend. I could tell that Sheryl and Ernie were concerned about me, but I ignored them. They couldn't even speak one work of Vietnamese. What business did they have taking in a kid when they couldn't even speak the same language? Why would Tha Huong send me to a town with no Vietnamese? I wanted to smash something, but I didn't own anything, so I couldn't do it.

When Monday came, I didn't want to go to school. Sheryl must have thought I was sick because she let me stay home. I spent most of the day walking around the yard breaking sticks. Eventually, my anger went away, and I just felt tired.

By the time Sheryl and Ernie got home, I was lying in bed shivering. My body hurt. I was exhausted, but I couldn't sleep. Sheryl brought me some chicken with dumplings, but the thought of eating made me feel nauseous. I wanted to just fall into a hole somewhere and never come out. That, really, was the lowest point in my life.

The next day, I didn't want to go to school again. Sheryl stayed home with me. She checked on me, sometimes sitting for a few minutes on the edge of the bed. After offering me some crackers at lunch time, she didn't come back for what seemed like a long time. I wondered if she had left me. Maybe she was calling Tha Huang so they would come to get me. The disappointment I felt at that thought surprised me. If I went back to Tha Huong, I would be with other Vietnamese. I could talk and play with people like me. But, I would miss Sheryl and Ernie, and David and Jeff. I would even miss Mr. Howard and Mr. Shredder.

That made me realize that, no matter how difficult it was going to be, I had to learn the language. Even though it wasn't a conscious decision, my mind, instinctively, knew that I had to block out Vietnam. If I didn't, I would never survive the homesickness and the changes of living in a different culture. And that's how I blocked my Vietnamese heritage.

I went through the empty house looking for Sheryl. I found her in the kitchen, heating a can of soup on the stove.

"Mom," I said. "Hungry."

"I'm fixing you something," she said.

I sat at the table, but she didn't turn around for a long time, just kept stirring the soup.

From that point on, *Sheryl* and *Ernie* were *Mom* and *Dad*.

Mom and Dad set me up with a tutor. I stayed after school every day until 5:00 or 5:30. The tutor was a teacher at the junior high. She broke up the alphabet, put words together, taught me everything. If I mispronounced something, she would make me say it again and again and keep doing it until I could say the word correctly. When we were finished, she would drive me home. She worked with me like that for two years.

She wasn't the only one to help me. My parents at home would encourage me to mimic sounds and pronounce phrases properly. I told Mom if I said something wrong to correct me. I wanted to be able to communicate. For me to understand things, I had to work hard, and it was great to gradually understand people. When I started holding actual conversations, I realized something important: *If you decide to do something, within your individual capabilities, your mind will make it happen.*

My friends helped me, too, although none of us realized it at the time. David's family and my family lived outside of Havana. His home was basically across the field and a forest away from me. For us to play together, he would just saunter across the field and vice versa. It wasn't but a five minute walk.

He must have called Jeff every time before he came, because inevitably, not long after he arrived, someone dropped Jeff off in my driveway. We didn't have cell phones back then, so when we were together, we would be out doing kid things. One of the first things David and Jeff taught me was how to dribble and shoot. When we got tired of playing basketball, we'd ride bikes. While we were playing, I was absorbing the language.

In a short time, I knew just enough English to be dangerous. Mom and Dad, their daughter Lauri, and I were sitting at home playing a board game. Lauri sent one of my pieces back to start, and I said, "I'm gonna kick your ass." They all burst out laughing. The laughter was so abrupt, I was scared. I didn't know *ass* was a bad word. I was just mimicking what I had heard at school. At that time, people didn't cuss in public, so, of course, they explained to me that "kick your butt" was a more sociably acceptable phrase to use.[5]

Learning that was good because about six

weeks after I enrolled in junior high, David and Jeff helped me sign up for the basketball team. For me, basketball practice meant a man yelling words I didn't understand and throwing folding chairs when the ball didn't go in the basket. In my eyes, the entire act was comical, but I didn't dare laugh. The other boys did their best to teach me the rules. I didn't care that I didn't play in any of the games; I just wanted to be part of the team.

After a few months, I could communicate enough that some of the teachers tried giving me tests. One day, the history teacher said, "Angel," as he gestured for me to follow him. *Angel* was a girl so quiet that, at first, I had thought she couldn't talk. She followed us to the empty room next door. The teacher laid a piece of paper on a desk, then left me alone with her. I watched her blonde hair sway around her petite face as she pronounced each word slowly, pointing as she went. She didn't talk loud like other people did; in fact, her voice was so quiet I almost couldn't hear her. As she read each choice under the sentence, she pointed to the letters, *a, b, c.* When she finished, she looked at me. I didn't know what I was supposed to do. She took the pencil and drew an imaginary circle around each letter, then handed the pencil back. I circled each letter.

She shook her head.

"No, circle one," she said, erasing my marks.

I understood *no, circle* and *one*, but I didn't understand why I was supposed to circle just one. When I circled the *b*, however, she smiled really big and nodded.

After that, I circled the *b* every time, gave her a huge smile, and waited for her to smile back at me. I would have circled *b*'s all day to see that smile.[6]

Word must have got around to the other teachers that Angel could "talk" to me because after that, every time there was a test, she and I would go to a different room so she could read to me. The first time I actually understood what I was supposed to do, I concentrated hard, trying to pick the correct answer. I knew I got it right when she said, "Yes," in a louder-than-usual voice. By Christmas break, I could answer at least some of the questions on the test.

I really enjoyed my first Christmas. In Vietnam, Christmas was solely a church celebration. We didn't exchange gifts or decorate. The artificial tree Mom put up in the living room fascinated me. After showing me how to hang ornaments, Mom gave me a box of blue globes. Carefully, I hung all of them on the same two branches, then stepped back, proud of the job I had done. Mom shook her head with a smile as she redistributed them.

On Christmas Eve, Mom and Dad invited some of the neighbors to supper. Little kids were everywhere. I wanted to disappear into my room, but Giang stayed, so I did. I didn't think it unusual when yet another visitor knocked.

"Hieu," Dad said, indicating that I needed to answer.

As I opened the door, a large man dressed all in red with a fluffy white beard stepped into the living room, simultaneously dropping a rough brown sack.

My first time meeting Santa AKA Uncle Bear

"Ho, Ho, Ho," he said in a deep, grandiose voice. "Merry Christmas!"

I expected Dad to sprint for his shotgun so he could make the intruder leave.

Instead, he said, "Well, hello, Santa,"

I had heard of Santa and knew he wasn't real. I didn't know people ran around impersonating him.

"Are there any good girls and boys here?" the burly man asked, looking at all of the kids who seemed to have frozen.

Some of them started screaming, "Me! Me! Me!" while jumping up and down. Others scrunched up tight against their moms, trying to hide their faces.

Dad offered his chair to this Santa man. Child after child went to sit on Santa's lap. Finally, a mom placed the smallest child in the chair with Santa. She immediately started bawling. All of the adults, including the Santa, burst out laughing.

Mom whipped out the camera. "Go stand by them, Hieu!"

I didn't understand why this character was so important, or why they wanted a picture of me with a kid sitting on his lap howling, but I did my best to smile as Mom snapped several pictures.

"I can't wait to get these back," she said, grinning. "I'm going to put a rush on the film development."

"Have you been a good boy, Hieu?" the man asked as he passed the screaming girl back to her mom.

Standing by the chair gave me a chance to examine him more closely. He looked a lot like Uncle Bear. He sounded like him, too. I had the almost irresistible urge to tug on the beard to see if it was real, but I knew that would be unthinkably rude.

"Answer Santa, Hieu," Dad encouraged me.

"Ya," I said.

"Well, Santa has some presents for you and the other kids," Santa said.

I continued to scrutinize him as he pulled wrapped gifts from his sack. I was more and more certain this was Uncle Bear. I wasn't sure why he was in disguise. I decided to ask Mom and Dad later what was going on.

The next day brought Lauri with more gifts. We sat by the tree the entire morning, unwrapping presents. The large sock they called a "stocking" was the strangest. I pulled gift after gift from its depths: socks and lip balm and a comb.

After Christmas, the school year went fast, and I was settling into life with the Laytons. I took helping around the house in stride, wanting to do my part, including help with the laundry. One boy the Laytons fostered had a different opinion.

After he had been at the house for a few days, mom showed him how to take the dirty clothes to the basement. However, he would throw his clothes down the stairs, leaving them scattered on the steps and floor.

Mom told him to pick up his clothes.

He said, "In Vietnam, men don't listen to women."

Mom said, "This isn't Vietnam, and you will listen to me."

Dad said, "You best listen to her."

After that, he did what Mom said.

Since I had only had a mother in Vietnam, having mom in charge didn't bother me. For me, it didn't matter who was in charge. Being here meant existing in an entirely different culture, and again, I went into survivor mode and blocked my Vietnamese background. I really didn't think about who was in charge. They told me to do something, and I just did it. It never entered my mind to rebel against Mom just because she was a woman.[7]

That summer, the other kids and I would get together in a field near my house to play baseball. Only one girl joined us: Tammy, a small girl with long blonde hair. She barely spoke, and I was still struggling with English, so I figured we would be a perfect match. David helped me write the note. "Dear Tammy, Would you be my girlfriend? Hieu."

David grinned as he delivered the note to Tammy's house. I watched him knock on the door. Her mom answered. The door closed, then opened. Tammy stood there, her blonde hair like a halo around her beautiful face. David handed her the piece of paper. She looked at it. The door closed as David came trotting back.[8]

"What did she say?" I asked anxiously.

"Sorry, Buddy," he said shaking his head.

"I'm never going to get a girlfriend," I said.

"Don't worry." David punched my arm. "I'll give you my leftovers."

That fall marked the beginning of my eighth grade year. Once again, I started out on the basketball team. One day, the coach called me over at the end of practice while the rest of the team went to change.

"Hieu." He spoke loudly and slowly as he put an arm around my shoulder. "I'm sorry, but you can't be on the team this year."

At first, I thought I had made a mistake about what he said. I shook my head. "I don't understand."

"You're too old to play on a junior high

team," he explained.

"What's 'too old'?" I asked.

"You're almost sixteen. That's too old for you to be on the team."

I was so upset that I didn't change. I just sat down on the bleachers and stared at the floor. When David came out, I couldn't look at him.

"What's wrong?" he asked.

I clenched my throat to keep my voice steady. I managed to say, "I can't play basketball."

He said, "What do you mean, you can't play basketball? You've been playing basketball. You're doing fine. "

"No, no, no, they won't let me play."

He sat next to me. "I don't understand what you're saying."

"Coach says I'm too old."

"Well, how old are you?" he asked.

As I told him, I came dangerously close to crying. My skill level wasn't the greatest, but I felt like a part of the team and what they were doing.

Dad talked with the coach. They called some places to clarify the rules. In the end, I was able to practice, but I wasn't allowed to play in the games. That was alright with me because I could still take part.[9]

This is the year Dad introduced me to hunting. He always wanted a boy to take hunting and fishing. When I got my first goose, Mom took pictures of me with it. Dad finally had somebody he could take with him to do all the guy things his daughters were never interested in doing. [10]

By the end of my eighth grade year, I had a fairly good grasp of the English language. I had the support of a new family, teachers, and friends. My courage and attitude made it easy for them to want to help me, but I had to have the determination and drive to succeed. I learned that *a person can have a world of help, but if that person isn't willing to work, the situation won't get any better.*

Every year at my school, the teachers picked a girl and a boy from the eighth grade class who embody everything that an American is supposed to be. That year, I was the boy selected for this award: the All-American Boy. As the award recipient, I had to give a speech at the eighth grade graduation. My English teacher helped me to write it. I was nervous about giving that speech, but I was also proud that I had been chosen.*

Eighth grade graduation marked a significant milestone in my life; perhaps more so than for other people. Up to this point, I had survived a terrible journey. I had learned a new language and acclimated to a new culture. Good people surrounded me, helping me on my way.

Eighth grade graduation giving the "All American Boy" speech.

In an interview, I summed up my experience thus far by saying, "I like being able to go anywhere I want to go and do anything I want to do."

*A copy of the speech appears after the last chapter of the book.

Chapter 6—Livin' the Dream

During the time I was in junior high and high school, the late '80's and early '90's, the culture of the United States retained a certain innocence based on mutual respect along with a measure of unselfishness. People felt good about helping each other. If a car broke down on the side of the road, people weren't afraid to help. Nobody locked their doors unless they were gone for more than an hour. The country was transitioning from the stay-at-home mom to the working mom as a societal norm. Kids rode their bikes around town without fear of being assaulted. Parents assumed that if their kid wasn't at home, he was at the neighbor's house. People smoked everywhere, but they didn't cuss in public.

Television stations broadcast programs with cussing or violence only after 8:00 p.m. when most children were in bed or headed in that direction. The main source of news came from the daily newspaper and from local television stations which broadcast news at 5:00 p.m. and 10:00 p.m. or from national news which broadcast weekdays at 7:00 a.m. and 5:30 p.m. Periodicals such as *U.S. News & World Report* and *Time Magazine*, which were delivered weekly, provided additional information for those who wanted more in-depth news.

The average American did not carry debt beyond a mortgage and perhaps a car loan. Most people used cash or wrote checks instead of using credit cards. When people went on vacation, they used traveler's checks. Most people didn't travel outside of the United States unless they were doing business or studying abroad.

Long distance telephone calls cost 10 cents a minute with a phone package; cell phones were just being introduced and their use was generally limited to businessmen in larger cities. Private phones were still attached to the walls; answering machines took messages when people didn't answer. Public bathrooms had bar soap—liquid soap was not commonly used at the time. *Starbucks* was not a household name. Kids didn't drink coffee. We mostly drank water. Bottled drinks such as soda were considered expensive and were only purchased for special occasions. This was the culture that influenced me during my first six years in the United States.

By the time I got to high school, I was one of the boys of Havana. The parents treated me like one of the kids. Never once did I feel like an outsider; I was a Mad Duck (the Havana school mascot). Not only did the Laytons raise me, Havana raised me. I am very thankful for that.

My core value system of respecting my parents and elders, always working for what I have, and not stopping until I overcome an obstacle defined my high school experience. This value system evolved from the early influence of Má, and the later influence of Mom and Dad. Throughout my high school years, I found that sticking firmly to my values helped people to trust me and helped me to trust myself. My values influenced me to make the right decision, no matter what the decision was. This consistency, again, helped me to garner trust from those around me.

A short time before I started my freshman year, the last boy the Laytons fostered came to live with us. Even though he would start school in the fall in the same class as me, he and I didn't have much in common. He couldn't speak much English; by that time my mind had entirely blocked the Vietnamese language. We each had our own room which gave less opportunities to interact than if we had shared a room. We naturally gravitated to different friend groups and didn't do a whole lot together.[1]

I didn't play football until high school. Butch Howarth (Coach Howarth) again played a major role in my life. This time, in sports. As soon as school started, he approached me about being part of the team. The coaches and other football players taught me how to play.

Before my friends had known me for very long, they realized that if I put my mind to anything, I would not stop until I finished it. Whatever I put my mind to, whatever I set as the goal, I would not stop until I reached that goal.

This was especially apparent to them in high school when we would work out. I was a strong kid, pound per pound. If I weighed 150 pounds, I could bench press double my weight, but that's because I wouldn't stop working until I got what I wanted.

Many times Jeff, David, and I were in the high school weight room, and Jeff and David would say, "Alright, that's good for today."

I would say, "No, we're not done with this set; we're not done with that rep."

Being high school kids, they would give me crap because I wouldn't let them stop a few reps short.

I'd say, "No, keep going, keep going."

They always finished the workout.

During my freshman and sophomore years, I played on the line, left guard. Defensively, I played middle linebacker. Our sophomore season, we were on the scout defense in football practice. We were practicing a pass play. Another player named Chase caught the ball as he came across the middle. David and I tackled him at the same time, BOOM, wrapped him up, took him down. After Chase got up, I was still lying on my back. David grabbed my hand. After I stood, he gave me a funny look.

He said, "Um, hey, you need to step out."

I said, "Why?"

He said, "I think your nose is broke."

Even though my nose was throbbing with pain, I said, "Nuh uh, no it's not."

He said, "Hey, man, your nose is crooked—like an *L*."

When I still refused to leave the practice, David motioned for a coach. "Hey, come here and check this out."

Coach Howarth walked over, took one look at my face, and said, "Oh, this ain't good."

I kept saying, "I'm fine, I'm fine."

I wanted to finish practice.

Another coach came over and said, "Nope, we need to send you to the emergency room. We need to get this checked out."

I said, "I'll go after practice."

The coaches said, "No, you're going now. "

So my parents took me to the emergency room.

I only missed a few practices the entire four years I played football. One of the practices I missed was because I had to get my nose reset.

We had a game on the following Monday night, a fresh-soph game. The team was sitting in the locker room, talking and just tossing the ball around. David went to toss it to me; the only problem was, I wasn't looking. It hit me right in the nose.

The pain that shot into my eyes, ignited an instinctual anger.

The reasonable part of my brain didn't see the kid who was my friend since I started school in America, it didn't see the guy who had supported and stood by me. In fact, the reasonable part of my brain took a step back and let the primitive side take over.

I grabbed ahold of David, simultaneously shoving him against the wall.

He said, "Man, it was an accident. I thought you were looking."

A couple of the other guys pulled me away from him. When they touched my arms, my reason returned, and I realized it was an accident.

I said, "Oh, sorry, sorry."

That's the only time I've ever been mad at him for something.

I know that he felt horrible. After that, I played with a shield over my face mask.[2]

Even though I was the oldest, Jeff got his license before David and I did— early in his sophomore year. Jeff would drive out to visit us. He had a Ford Ranger, and you'd see the three of us crammed into it. We drove "The Square." The route was over Dearborn Hill, around Hardee's, come back out, take a left on Schrader, take a right on Main Street, and then come back up Promenade to Dearborn. That was the big square. You had to drive it both directions. You'd go one way one time and one way the other just in case somebody was going the same direction you were. That way you'd see who was out and about. You had to make the circle around Hardee's. I don't know how that got implemented, but the Hardee's parking lot was the main hang-out. You didn't hang out at Hardees too long, maybe thirty minutes or so.

By my junior year, I had my driver's license, and a pick-up truck that I bought from a cousin. That was important because in the fall of 1993, Havana experienced a 100 year flood. That year, the Mississippi and Missouri rivers flooded. Havana is built over a natural aquifer. The aquifer reached peak capacity, and the overflow seeped up through the ground, flooding many parts of the town. Highway 97 going into Havana was closed for a time, and the schools flooded. I hauled all kinds of dirt and sand bags with my truck to help the schools put up a barricade to stop the water flowing into the buildings.[3]

When I was a junior, I started football with the varsity team, same position, left guard, and middle linebacker. I played alongside my two best friends. Jeff was the left tackle. We lined up next to each other. David was quarterback. We always had fun playing with each other.

An incident that happened during my junior year shows how important my values were and how far I had come in the understanding of the English language. That year, I took English III. The teacher emphasized writing. The entire year, our class was either writing or revising an essay at all times. Since computers weren't widely in use at that time, we wrote everything except our research papers, by hand.

One day, my English teacher asked me to stay after class. She showed me my latest essay, and the essay of one of my classmates. Although written in our individual handwriting, the essays were virtually the same, word-for-word.

I could tell she was uncomfortable with the situation.

She said, "Hieu, one of you cheated. Your English skills are far superior to the other student's writing, so unless he confesses, I can't rule out the possibility that you let him copy your paper."

I was immediately insulted that she would even consider that I would cheat.

I said, "I don't cheat."

She said, "Unless he confesses, I have to give you both zeros."

This was unfair. I didn't understand why she had to give both of us zeros. I left the classroom disgruntled and angry at her and at my friend.

The next day in class, I was still angry with her. However, one of my core values is to respect my elders and those in authority over me. I didn't give her any dirty looks, and I made sure to speak to her in a pleasant tone.

When I got home that day, I found out that she had called my parents about it. They talked to me about the rule and about why she had to give us both zeros. I understood a little better, but I still thought it was unfair.

The next day, she again kept me after class.

"Hieu," she said. "I spoke to the other student's parents. They talked to their son, and he confessed to cheating."

After that, I was careful to keep my papers where my classmates couldn't see them.

Even though that time worked out for me, Jeff and David made sure I got at least a warning from the teachers on a regular basis. They had a thing where if one of us would sit behind the other one in class, they'd flick the one in front's ear. And if they did it just right, they'd be able to flick it when the teacher didn't see it.

They loved to get me because I would always get mad. I'd turn around and say something.

Then the teacher would say, "Hieu, would you face forward?"

I'd get so mad at them for flicking my ear.

I did, however, make sure there was payback for all of the trouble.

I'd always eat at David's house, or he would always eat at mine. Our refrigerator was always open to my friends. The three of us, David, Jeff, and I, were eating a leftover chicken dinner at my house one day, and David started rummaging through our refrigerator. He saw some green vegetables in a jar.

He said, "Hey, can I have some of these green beans?"

I just kept eating and said casually, "Yeah, Yeah, go ahead."

David asked, "What are they?"

I said, "Those are Vietnamese green beans. Those are good."

He said, "Oh, ok."

So he put two of 'em on his plate.

He looked at the long green vegetables suspiciously and said, "They're not hot are they?"

I said, "No, no, no, they're good; they're good."

David took about a two-three inch bite out of one. After one chomp, he immediately ran to the sink. His mouth was on fire. They had some hot pepper spices in them. Jeff and I were on the floor laughing.

I said, "Those aren't Vietnamese green beans."

I always liked hot foods, and I loved to trick my friends into trying some of my spicier choices.[4]

Our senior year, the three of us could have our pick of positions on the football team. I wanted to run the ball, and Jeff wanted to catch the ball.

One day, Coach Howarth called Jeff and me

in to his office.

He said, "Look, I know these are the positions you want, but we're short on offensive linemen. I need you in the line blocking. You'll never get your name announced over the intercom, it's a no-name position of just blocking for David. Since you both are seniors, it's your call. If you want to run and catch, I'll make sure you get to do that."

Jeff and I looked at each other.

He said, "Hey, man, I don't care about having my name announced."

I said, "Me, neither."

We shook coach's hand.

So, we made one side of the line. David was the quarterback; he ran behind us all of the time. It was great. I was just happy to be out there. Ironically, I was voted "All Conference" that year and received a certificate at our athletic banquet.

On our ride, home after one particular game-- I can't remember whether we won or lost-Coach Howarth and I were sitting on the bus together talking. By this time, I felt like he was a mentor to me, so I was comfortable telling him the story of me coming over on the boat. ". It was dark on the bus, so I don't think he knew I could see him wiping his eyes while I was talking. He kept saying that he didn't realize what I had been through.[5]

During my senior year, the blonde-haired girl, Angel, came back into my life when we took a class together: Vietnam History. I enrolled in the class thinking it was going to be an easy *A*. Ironically, since I had basically blocked my Vietnamese experience, I had no idea what the whole class was about. Every week, on Monday, the class would get this worksheet, answer the questions from the chapter, and then on Friday, we could use our notes to take the test. David, Jeff, and I would go over to Angel's house on Thursday night to copy the notes so we could pass the test. In the fall, there was always a football game on Friday. Angel's dad would get us all riled up for football.[6] We weren't dating then, but it reintroduced her to me on a more than casual acquaintance basis, which set the stage for the Homecoming dance.

In small towns in the early nineties, one football game, usually in late October, was designated as the Homecoming game. The athletic director tried to schedule this game against a team at the playing level of our team or a little below so we at least had a chance of winning. The entire week before the big game was devoted to Homecoming activities. Every class had a committee that met after school each night to stuff colored tissue paper into miles of chicken wire to decorate a float according to the Homecoming theme.

A few weeks before Homecoming, the high school students elected one boy and one girl from the freshman, sophomore, and junior classes to the Homecoming court. They chose four boys and four girls from the senior class. During Homecoming week, the students chose a king and queen from the elected seniors; the winners were announced at a pep rally prior to the Homecoming parade. According to tradition, each couple on the court, freshman through senior, rode in the Homecoming parade on the back of a convertible. Seniors not voted to be king or queen were randomly paired to ride together. Angel and I were elected to the Homecoming court our senior year; we were also paired to ride together in the Homecoming parade.

Angel and me riding in the Homecoming parade.

I went to the dance with a girl who was also friends with Angel; Angel went to the dance with other friends. After the dance, I took the girl home, then went to a get-together that Angel happened to be attending. Angel and I started dating that night, but we broke up after a few weeks. I regretted breaking up with Angel almost immediately, but I didn't know how to get the relationship started again.

Since we were both involved in many school activities, we still saw each other, mainly when we were with the Peer Facilitators. The purpose of this group was to provide leadership and mentors to the younger children in the school district. During our junior year of training, our sponsor, Brenda Stadsholt, emphasized bonding, speaking our minds, and keeping things confidential within the group. During our senior year, we used what we learned. We would go over to New Central, the elementary school, so we could tutor children by working with students who had reading problems or help the staff by putting up bulletin boards. We did whatever the elementary teachers asked us to do.

During the time of Peer Facilitators, we started a blood drive for the high school. Until then, if you wanted to donate blood as a high school student, you weren't able to unless you did it on your own. At that time, the Church of Christ held regular blood drives. The other peer facilitators and I, along with Mrs. Stadsholt, worked with the local blood drive coordinators to get the high school involved in the blood drive. For two years our sponsor, along with some other adults, would use the Stadholts' van to bus the high school kids back and forth to the Church of Christ to donate blood.

We also worked on the daffodil project, also called Daffodil Days, which was for cancer research. We sold daffodils in the winter and delivered them in the spring. The profits from the sales went to cancer research.

Every year, this group sold suckers and candy bars and all sorts of things to earn money to go to Chicago on a field trip. Mrs. Stadsholt told us, "I was cheer sponsor, so I've ridden too many school buses. If you want to take a trip, I'm not going to ride a school bus, so you have to earn enough money to take a charter bus." [7] We didn't want to ride a school bus all the way to Chicago, either, so we were always motivated in our sales.

Even though we saw each other in Peer Facilitators and every day in the hall at school, I felt awkward approaching Angel until I was sure she was open to seeing me again. Sometime in February, I started playing the "telephone game." Angel was friends with a girl named Lisa. I would talk to Lisa who would then relay what I wanted to say to Angel. She told me whatever Angel said. We officially started dating again in February at Lisa's birthday party.

Right around prom, we started getting serious. I knew she was the one. Since I wanted to be able to support my wife and children, I told Angel that we would have to wait until I had a steady income before we made anything official. I wasn't sure she was willing to wait that long, or if our relationship would weather the upcoming years of change, but I decided that if we broke up, then it wasn't meant to be.

Senior Prom

I graduated from high school in May of 1994.

I had worked for the past seven years to learn the American culture and the English language; I had spent four of those years working to achieve a high school diploma. I wasn't sure what I wanted to do after high school, but I was already working toward the biggest goal of my life: to become an American citizen.

Chapter 7—Goals

Shortly before I graduated from high school, Dad said, "Son, you have two options. You can get a job or go to college, but you are not going to sit around doing nothing."

"I'm not sure what to do," I told him.

"Why don't you go to Bloomington or Peoria and apply for a job?" he suggested.

So I went to Bloomington. I applied for a job anyplace that would take my application. I applied to several insurance agencies. I even went to the I.A.A. building, Country Financial's corporate headquarters. I'm not sure what I thought they would hire me to do. I guess I thought, "Maybe I'll get lucky or something."

A couple of weeks later, I didn't hear from anyone besides Country Financial. They sent me a letter. In short it said, "Son, you need more education."

By this time, Jeff was the only one of the three of us friends who knew what he was going to do. MacMurray had chosen him to play on their football team. David was waiting to hear from two colleges about baseball scholarships.

One day, David and I were sitting at his

house, eating snacks and watching television.

Out of the blue, David said, "Alright, if I don't hear within two days from these two schools, we'll join the military."

I said, "OK."

It sounded like a good idea at the time.

"Which one are we going to join?"

"I don't know, Army?"

"I don't know man, the Marines have a better uniform and better commercials on TV. Let's go with them."

I gave him a high-five. "OK, let's do it."

Two days later, we were hanging out at Jeff's house when David's mom called. Jeff and I didn't take our eyes off the television while he was in the kitchen talking to her.

When he flopped back onto the couch, he announced, "It looks like I'm going to go to Lincoln to play baseball on scholarship."

I still wasn't sure about my plans, but since my friends were going to college, I figured I might as well send in some applications. Ironically, I asked my English III teacher to write a letter of recommendation for me.

That summer, I was accepted by Monmouth College, it's an NCAA Division III private school.

Since I had never been there, I decided to visit. Angel went with me. She was considering several options from attending the local junior college to enrolling in the four-year university close by. During our campus tour, she decided to go to Monmouth, too.

Over the course of the time I had been in America, I formed a vision of what I wanted my working life to look like. In this vision, I had an office with a secretary. I didn't know what I would be doing in that office, but that was my dream. With that in mind, I chose to work toward a degree in business. Initially, I also took classes toward a minor in computer science, but the classes were difficult for me. Since having a computer science minor would not affect achieving my ultimate goal, I decided to drop it so I could focus on doing well in my main area of study.

In addition to attending classes at Monmouth, I played football there for one year. As I practiced, I came to realize: I was big and strong, but there were bigger and stronger guys out there. All I was doing was getting sore. I knew that I wasn't going to go any further with football, so I decided to stop playing so that I could focus on my education. During this time, I faced two road blocks to my success, one was natural, and one was of my own doing. Angel worked beside me so that I could overcome both of them. The first road block was my writing ability. Like many people, I struggled with writing. Fortunately, Angel was there. She helped me along the way by proofreading my papers. The second road block was my penchant to party, hard.

Almost from the first day of college, I started to go to parties where I drank heavily. By the middle of my sophomore year, my grades started to drop to the point that I was on academic warning. Angel told me that if I didn't stop, she was going to break up with me. That caused me to realize that my drinking had become a problem. I didn't stop partying altogether, but I did stop drinking too much at a time. Consequently, my grades went back up. I am fortunate that Angel loved me enough to be honest with me and to separate herself from me if I didn't stop my destructive behavior. I decided that I wanted to surround myself with those types of people in the future: people who cared enough about me to be honest with me, even if what they had to say could potentially damage our relationship. I also vowed that I would never resent a friend's honesty about one of my flaws.

During my sophomore year, two important events happened. First, I went to get my citizenship. I had been told there would be tests: the written test, verbal test, all kinds of tests. I went in for the interview. I didn't have to do any other tests. I became an American citizen on November 22, 1995. It was a proud day. A day that opened fresh possibilities for attaining the American Dream.

Havana's Hieu Tran sworn in as U.S. citizen

Article printed in the Mason County Democrat
in Havana, IL

The second important event happened while I was playing video games. I was in the basement because at that time, only wealthy students had computers in their rooms, and it was the full set with the large tower and monitor. People working in businesses were the only ones using laptops. Many students didn't even have televisions in their rooms. We could rent a video game console from the front desk which we could hook up to the television in the basement lounge. We could also rent video games from the front desk or from a local video store.

At the time of this big event. I was flopped on the couch in the downstairs lounge playing video games on the rented console.

My roommate popped his head in.

He said, "Hieu, you've got a phone call. It's your mom."

Since cell phones still weren't in wide use at this time, I could only take the call if I hauled my butt upstairs to talk on the phone attached to the wall of my dorm room. Talking to my mom wasn't worth stopping in the middle of a game I'd spent 50 cents to rent. If I left, I also risked losing my spot on the couch along with use of the television. I waved to him over the back of the couch. "Yeah, let me finish this game."

He said, "Hieu, no, you've got a phone call from your mom."

I said, "Yeah, let me finish this game. I'll call her."

He said, "No, your mother from Vietnam."

I felt like somebody had just punched me in the gut. I hadn't communicated with her since I was in Peoria. Two years of junior high, four years of high school, and almost two years of college had passed since our last correspondence.

I was sweating so bad for the next half an hour that I didn't know what to do. I answered the phone and listened to her voice. It was like she was sitting right next to me. I could understand a few things that she said, but I couldn't communicate with her. All the memories came back. I wanted to tell her how much I missed her, how much I wanted her to be here to see me, but I couldn't. All I could do was make noises so she would know I was listening.

After our conversation, I realized that in the effort to survive all that I had been through, my mind had blocked out the Vietnamese language. I felt so frustrated. So much had happened in my life that I wanted to tell her. The most important thing that I wanted to tell her was that I was alright. I was in America. I was in college--which was unheard of for my family. I wanted to talk to Má.

One of the first things I did after the call was to let my mom and dad (Sheryl and Ernie) know. A lot of foster parents, or adopted parents, don't want their foster children to reconnect with their biological families because of jealousy, but not the Laytons. They encouraged me to reconnect with Má.

In order to do that, I had to come up with a strategy to relearn the Vietnamese language. First, I started going to the library regularly to read a Vietnamese to English dictionary with phonetic pronunciations. Second, I went through the college directory to find other Vietnamese students. After I told them a little bit of my story, I asked if they would meet with me to practice speaking Vietnamese. After a surprisingly short time, the language started to come back.

Má continued to call. We were able to catch up on what was going on with each other. The most amazing thing she told me was how she found me. In this pre-Internet society, she decided to hire a private investigator. They tracked me down to Monmouth and got my phone number.

Christmas of my junior year, Mom and Dad gave me the money to buy a plane ticket to go to Vietnam for thirty days. That was huge. They took me to the airport knowing in their minds that I might decide not to come back, knowing that I was going to what was a foreign country to me, knowing that I didn't know how to speak Vietnamese well at all. It was great not only that they made it possible for me to do that but also that they gave me the complete freedom to do it.

First time I reunited with my mom when
I was in college.

When I landed, I was scared. The flight wasn't difficult because I flew from Chicago to Korea to Ho Chi Minh City (formerly Saigon); all along the way, everyone spoke English. That's one good thing about speaking English; there's English in all of the world's major cities. Once I arrived in Vietnam, once I walked inside Ho Chi Minh City Airport, I became just a little fish in a big pond.

Má was there waiting.

As I looked around, I heard her voice calling to me. I am telling you that once you hear your mom's voice, no matter how old you are, you remember it.

She chartered a motor vehicle to transport us the four hours to her house. I experienced culture shock because I was accustomed to a mostly white population, and when we left the airport, there were Vietnamese people everywhere. The Vietnamese everyone spoke was much too fast. Anyone who conversed with me had to speak slowly with a more formal Vietnamese because I couldn't understand the slang. Even then, I had to translate what they said to English and then translate my answer back into Vietnamese. After a while, my head hurt. As we drove, I remembered everything I saw, but it seemed so small now. When I lived here, I thought the city had the greatest things, but now, I saw the need for improvement. I was used to cars going fifty-five miles an hour in the United States versus about ten miles an hour in Vietnam. It was like traveling thirty years back in time.

The next day when I woke up on a bamboo mat in a tiny hut, it really sank in that I was back in my childhood home. I had forgotten the shrine to my father in the corner of the hut. It was still there, hanging on the wall over a shelf holding fruits like oranges: a crudely drawn picture of a man that represented my biological father. When I asked about him, the answer was the same as before I left. She did light candles to honor him one evening after we finished supper.

Má insisted on doing everything for me. It didn't matter that I was a grown man; she had her little boy back. She was still the same touchy feely person. She rubbed my legs, my arms, my back. Once in a while, she took out her fan to give me some air, just as she had done so many years ago. One way she showed love was to make food, which she encouraged me to eat. For one meal, I found a fish head in my bowl. I was about to throw it out when Má stopped me. The fish head was considered the best part of the meal, so even though I didn't want to, I ate it. I forgot that Má didn't waste anything. The Vietnamese people eat fish and chicken until the bones are clean without a scrap of meat. They just don't have the resources we do, so they use every little bit of food.

Most of our conversations involved just talking to get to know each other better; however, some of our conversations turned more serious.

Má would look me straight in the eye. "Don't

smoke, don't drink, and don't beat your wife."

The first time she said this to me, I was speechless. I didn't smoke. I had quit getting drunk. It had never occurred to me that I would beat my wife when I got married. I realized that she didn't really know any different. In Vietnam, men beat their wives. She assumed that men in America did the same.

I tried to explain to her, but she just kept emphasizing not to do those things.

"Another thing," she inevitably went on to say, "don't get divorced. All those Americans do is divorce. They jump from wife to wife like this," she snapped her fingers. "You marry somebody, you stay with her."

"I will," I promised.

I didn't tell her about Angel. She would have been horrified that I was dating a white woman. Her son being married to a different race would be significant for her. Even though she hadn't been a part of my life for almost ten years, she expected me to marry a Vietnamese girl.

Marriage was important to my mom. Even though it wasn't a crime, Vietnamese society looked down on remarrying. Vietnamese society expected each person to marry only once. If a woman

105

remarried as a widow, it wouldn't have been frowned upon like a divorce would have, but Vietnamese society expected a widow to be committed to her dead husband for the rest of her life. She never told me why she chose not to find another husband, but in my heart, I really think that she was just dedicated to my dad. Telling her that I planned to marry a white woman would have ruined the entire visit for both of us.

After I had been there for a month, I had to leave again. I saw how devastated she was. I couldn't imagine how bad it was for her the first time I left as a kid.

Talking to Má prompted me to think seriously about having my own family after I got back to the States. I decided to propose to Angel. Having family around to witness this great event was important to me. I called mom and dad and Angel's parents, as well as Lauri, Uncle Bear, and a few others to set a date for the proposal.

When the big day came, Angel had no idea of what was about to happen. I told her that I wanted to see my mom and dad. As we drove to Havana, the ring was in the console between us in my truck. I was really nervous, but Angel didn't catch on until we got to the house. A lot of cars were parked in the driveway and along the road.

Before we got out of the truck, Angel asked, "What is going on?"

"I don't know," he said. "I guess our families decided to come over to see us."

Everybody greeted us, and thankfully, acted normal. I decided to ask her right away.

I led her by the hand to the middle of the living room. The family circled around us.

I got down on one knee. "Angel, would you marry me?"

She said, "Yes," right away.

We went to a local restaurant for supper. We saw mutual friends a couple of times while we were eating. Angel was really quiet; she didn't show any of them the ring.

On the way home, I wondered if she was having second thoughts about us getting married, so I asked her, "Why didn't you show them the ring?"

She said, "I don't know, I think I was just in shock."

Once we started talking about wedding plans, she got excited, so I knew she wanted to marry me.

Even though I talked regularly to Má, I put off telling her about my engagement. The ensuing argument was something I wanted to avoid for as long as possible. I didn't tell Angel about Má's expected objections to our marriage. This was a battle I had to fight for myself, and there was nothing Angel could do to help.

My senior year flew by. Dad told me to start looking for employment in the Spring. I went to job fairs but didn't have any luck in procuring even an interview.

I graduated from Monmouth in May of 1998 with a Bachelor of Arts degree in business administration with a minor in economics. Graduating from college would have been impossible if I had remained in Vietnam. Ten and a half years of hard work had brought me from abject poverty to being an American citizen with a college degree and a promising future. I had not only realized my dream, I had realized my family's dream. A dream that began roughly thirty-eight years before.

Monmouth College Graduation with mom and dad.

Chapter 8—The Mysterious Soldier

Seeing Má caused me think back to when she let me go. I realized that my defining question was formed long before I was born, in the history of my native country, Vietnam. Many people only know Vietnam through limited knowledge of a brief time labeled as the *Vietnam War*. However, only knowledge of Vietnam's centuries old history could give true shape to the events that brought me to that night.

Conflict forged Vietnam into the country it is today. China greatly influenced its people by ruling the area until 1010A.D. [1] when "The Ly princes" seized control. Subsequently, warring tribes exchanged power over the land, from generation to generation,[2] until France decided to conquer what was then known as *Indo China*: modern day *Cambodia, Laos,* and *Vietnam.*[3] In 1858, France established colonial rule.[4] They maintained this jurisdiction until World War II when Japan pushed in to occupy Vietnam alongside them.[5] At the end of World War II, a strong Vietnamese leader emerged: Ho Chi Minh. The Japanese withdrew. In 1946, an agreement awarded Ho Chi Minh rule over some

Northern Vietnamese land with France occupying the rest.[6] For the next eight years Ho Chi Minh's army struggled to establish dominion over the territories ruled by France. [7] In 1954, the French decided to withdraw from Vietnam. Under "the 1954 Geneva treaty"[8] land north of the 17th parallel became communist. Land to the south was democratic.[9] Communist take-over of Vietnam set the first great diaspora in motion, a time "during which over one million people"[10] moved south to escape the harsh consequences of Ho Chi Minh's rule.[11] Less than ten years later, the Vietnam War began.

These events molded my family's past as well as formed their dreams for the future. However, I had questions that the history of my first family's people, the Vietnamese people, didn't answer. For that, I needed to dig deeper into the papers which had traveled with me on that treacherous journey a decade before. I had them stored in a box somewhere. When I read through them, I discovered questions that were asked and answered at the same time, and the reason I was able to choose any place in the world that I wanted to go. Careful perusal of the information led me to a mysterious soldier, someone I had known about for my entire life, but someone I hadn't known at all.

The mysterious soldier was born on June 20, 1938.[12] Although I am not sure whether his family was originally from North or South Vietnam, he was seventeen at the time of the first great diaspora, which made him old enough to have clear memories of the much-despised French rule of his country.[13] During this first diaspora, the Vietnamese people were given a few months to decide where to live, in North or South Vietnam.[14] The soldier's family was most likely among them.

On November 20, 1960, with the build-up of hostilities, the young man recognized the threat of communist take-over of South Vietnam. Therefore, at age twenty-three, he left a life of farming to enlist in Vietnam's *Civil Guard* [15] later known as the *Regional Forces*. The Regional Forces protected the villages from the Viet Cong.[16] The mysterious soldier's decision to join the Regional Forces came as a result of gradual escalation in fighting between North and South Vietnam. This soldier, like most Vietnamese people, had a fierce love of his country. First, and foremost, he wanted Vietnam to be ruled by Vietnamese people. Second, and of equal importance, he wanted Vietnam to be a democracy. Since the time the communist leader Ho Chi Minh took full control of North Vietnam, news of executions and atrocities reached South Vietnam on a daily basis from those fortunate enough to escape across the 17th parallel. The mysterious soldier did not want the people of South Vietnam to suffer a similar fate. Since his unit was maybe ten miles from a military hot spot,[17] he enlisted fully aware that he may be called to give his life for his country.

Five and a half years later, on June 1, 1965, he was promoted to Corporal; two and a half years after that, on January 1, 1968, he was promoted to First Corporal.[18] This promotion occurred in a month the Viet Cong had proposed for a cease fire so that the Vietnamese people could celebrate Tet, the Vietnamese New Year.

With the threat of violence from the North momentarily abated, he and his buddies took turns visiting relatives, always leaving a skeleton crew to watch over the command post. Since the soldier's parents had died, he most certainly celebrated at least a part of this particular Tet with his brother's family. To prepare the family feast, his brother's wife and daughters wrapped leaves around square rice cakes stuffed with cooked bean paste and ground meat before steaming them to make *Bang Chung*. Other dishes included *Xôi Gấc* (red sticky rice), mung bean pudding, and pickled onions. This food must have been a welcome relief from the everyday meals of a bachelor soldier. More importantly, this time allowed him to join other family members to honor his parents and other dead ancestors, which is extremely important to the Vietnamese people.[19]

Sometime during the week-long celebration, on the morning of January 30, 1968, the mysterious soldier was sleeping on a mat in a hut crowded with his brother's family when he heard the sounds of gunfire. He wouldn't know until later that General Giap, commander of the Northern Army, had launched a massive, surprise attack on South Vietnam. Popping noises and screams accompanied by men, women, and children running in all directions caused him to grab his M2 carbine and kneel at the entrance to the hut. When he saw that his brother's family was in no immediate danger, he disappeared into the chaos to join his comrades in fighting off the North Vietnamese aggressors. By defending the territory, the soldier joined his countrymen and American soldiers in fighting the most widespread and bloodiest battle of the Vietnam War.[20]

After the South Vietnamese and American forces stopped the Tet Offensive, the soldier realized that the escalation in the war meant it would not be over soon. He was thirty-one years old with no children. This, coupled with his recent promotion, prompted him to consider finding a wife.

I am not sure how the soldier met Má, but their marriage was almost certainly a traditional one arranged by Má parents. Her mom and dad probably knew his mom and dad before they died, and there may have been an understanding between the two sets of parents which dated to their teenage years. Má married the soldier on June 2, 1968. The mysterious soldier's name was Tran Em. He was my father.[21]

Six weeks after the marriage, my father reenlisted in the army on July 24, 1968.[22] He had served eight years, and certainly could have returned to farming, but he knew that each person's contribution to the war effort mattered. For him, quitting the military would mean surrendering to the communist threat. Since my father was a member of the Regional Forces, he remained close to where Má lived even as he fought the North Vietnamese threat. Soldiers stationed near their families could make frequent visits so that their families could provide food and supplies. [23]

After they married, my father moved Má into one of the strategic hamlets, which were living areas designed by President Diem with the help of the

American government. Strategic hamlets were villages enclosed in fences with barbed wire. Guard towers provided surveillance of the surrounding countryside. "Bamboo spikes" driven into the banks of "moats" surrounding the fence were devised to give added security. These hamlets were supposed to be safe places for the South Vietnamese farmers to reside, protected from the Viet Cong.

By the time my parents married, the hamlet project had been deemed a failure; [24] nevertheless, Má resided in Bao Hoa hamlet until after the war. I don't know for sure why Má consented to live there. Due to its location near an American army base, it may have been one of the more successful hamlets. Additionally, since the Regional Forces there were strong in the area, the families may have accepted the hamlet program more readily, and the Viet Cong may not have infiltrated it.

Between the time of their marriage and 1972, Má had four children, Tran Thi Nga, a little girl born on May 24, 1969; Tran Van Tuyen, a baby boy, born on May 26, 1970; Tran Loan, a baby girl, born on June 4, 1971; and Tran Thi Nhung, a baby girl born on March 8, 1972. Of those children, my sister Loan was the only one to survive. [25]

On June 1, 1972, just three months after the

birth of his fourth child, my father was promoted to Sergeant. He had received the DP Award 4th class, maybe as a result of his actions during Tet. Almost a year later, on April 1, 1973, he was assigned command of a platoon. Shortly thereafter on September 24, 1973, he began non-commissioned officer's training, at Van Kiep,[26] an Australian training facility run by the Australian military. While he was there, my father learned the Australian methods of jungle warfare.[27]

My father has one discipline note in his records. He was absent without leave from October 6, 1973, to October 8, 1973. He received one day of close confinement when he returned. I believe he went to see Má. He had been at Van Kiep for less than two weeks of the six week course. Something urgent must have caused him to go AWOL. Since the fighting was getting closer, my father may have wanted to visit his family one last time. He and Má may have made plans in the case of his death or communist takeover. On December 22, 1973, my father finished his training at Van Kiep and returned to his former unit.[28]

My father's last visit was when he came to see me after I was born in April of 1974. Má told me that he stayed for four days and held me for much of that time. After that, he returned to his unit.

Má never spoke of my father except to say he was a military guy, a soldier and that he went away on a mission and never returned. He was recorded missing in combat on May 28, 1974.[29] One of my father's friends brought the news of his death to Má; he told her that my father blew up. He brought my father's personal effects including his watch. That is the most certainty we have of his death without actually seeing a body.

Almost a month to the day after my father's death, the military sent Má a letter declaring him MIA. The letter is addressed to Wife Tran Thi Lua, Bao Hoa Hamlet. It reads in part:

Date, location, and reason of missing: on 16:30 date April 28, 1974, at YT. 466894 area of Xuan Loc Long Khanh, the operation contacted with Vietnamese Communist armed forces and he was missed in duty.[30]

The plastic sack Má taped to my chest contained a copy of this letter along with my father's military service record, a record of the compensation package Má received from the government, and my birth certificate. Because my father fought alongside the American soldiers, I had my own cabin on the cargo ship, moved through the Singapore refugee camp faster than other people, and was offered the choice of living anyplace in the world.

My father was a brave man who believed in freedom. He continued to fight for South Vietnam after the American soldiers pulled out, when the communist takeover was almost certain. If he had remained alive after Ho Chi Minh took control, he could have been imprisoned, executed, or our entire family could have been killed. My family's dreams of America were rooted in my father's undefeatable desire for freedom and his unwavering refusal to compromise his beliefs, even though it meant dying for what he believed.

Chapter 9—Lua Tran the Secret Keeper

While I was learning about my father, I was piecing together Má's story. By remembering stories she and my relatives had told, reading through the papers, and remembering what I could from my childhood, I was able to reconstruct what Má's life had been like.

Before the communist takeover of South Vietnam, Má's personality leaned toward the easygoing openness of a person without fear. She married a good man and had healthy children. The land Má inherited from her parents provided enough income for food, clothing, and shelter. The United States sent troops to fight alongside her husband and the other South Vietnamese soldiers; this meant the communists would stay North. All of this ensured the future that Má wanted: a happy time full of sons and grandsons.

After the communist takeover, Má became quiet, reserved, and always alert, like a person in constant danger. My father's death, the United States withdrawal from the war, and the eventual communist rule brought fear, and secrets. Má's secrets kept guard over her mouth. They made her careful and cunning and brave. Her undisclosed information focused her actions toward one goal: escaping to America.

After my father died, Má went to the government to get his paperwork in order. This was before the communist takeover of South Vietnam. The South Vietnamese government gave compensation to every soldier's widow. On the papers, Má claimed five living children; three of those children died before I was old enough to remember. She never spoke of them. The government allotted her a sum of $249,600 which was to be distributed to her in even payments over the course of twelve months. Since this paperwork became official in July of 1974, [1] and Saigon fell on April 30, 1975, she probably didn't receive the full amount. She immediately converted the payments she did receive to gold along with procuring multiple copies of the government paperwork documenting my father's service and the details of our family.

When Saigon fell, Má moved to Phú Lâm, a community a small distance from her rice field. Doing so protected her from the coming communist takeover in many ways. First, it separated her from any neighbors who knew her background, particularly that her husband had fought with the Americans. Since there were no computers then, it was easier to maintain a certain degree of anonymity. Second, it made her appear poorer than she actually was. The communists despised landowners and anyone who appeared to make or have more money than others. While working in the rice paddy, she would appear to be a poor peasant eking out a meager living on whatever she could grow. While at home, she would appear to be a poor peasant barely able to afford anything more than a mud hut with a grass roof and a hole in the ground for a toilet. She buried the gold, and my father's paperwork, in the dirt floor of the hut, then placed her three cooking rocks over it to mark the spot and to obscure any suspicious unevenness in the hard packed dirt. After this, Má insisted that someone always had to be at the "house." She taught Chị and me that this kept thieves from stealing her cooking pot and the chickens and pig we kept in the yard. What we really protected was much more valuable. With this accomplished, she worked and waited.

Escaping to America was never a game to Má. When she said good-bye to me on the night I left, she knew from experience how tough it would be. Má's family originally lived in North Vietnam. Hard working people who believed in being frugal, her parents converted any money they could save into gold or land. In Vietnam at this time there were two major religions: Buddhism and Catholicism; Má's family was Catholic. Once a week, the women traded their loose fitting work clothes for more formal dresses, and the men put on their best shirts and pants so they could attend Mass at the nearby church. The church and the land were the center of their lives.

Má's birthdate is October 25, 1945[2]. Eight years later, in 1954, when France withdrew completely from Vietnam, Má's family was faced with a difficult decision. They were on the Northern side of the seventeenth parallel which the peace treaty placed as a boundary between Northern and Southern Vietnam. If they stayed with their family land, they would be ruled by communist Ho Chi Minh. If they moved south, they would have to start from scratch, but would be in a democratic country led by Bao Dai and Ngo Dinh Diem. My grandparents had less than a year to decide since the Geneva Accords provided nine months of safe passage over the parallel for anyone who wanted to relocate.[3]

My grandparents, like many others, probably moved south immediately since they, especially, would have been a target for this new government. They were land owners, and under communist rule, "anyone owning more than an acre of land could be brought to a people's tribunal." [4] Má's family was also devoutly Catholic. Again, Catholics faced persecution by the communists.[5]

Understanding the Vietnamese culture conveys a sense of the absolute terror necessary to uproot families from their land. My grandparents had lived in the same village for generations.

My grandfather viewed the land as a sacred trust he had received from his father so that he could pass it down to his oldest son. Leaving it was like having a piece of the very fabric of his existence torn away.

When they migrated, Má's family probably took advantage of traveling on one of the ships provided by sympathetic countries to transport North Vietnamese to South Vietnam.[6] Since Má's family most likely had invested much of their money in gold, they easily transported their wealth and reinvested in the land which was readily available in South Vietnam. Má was around eight years old at the time of this great migration.

Adapting to the South Vietnamese culture would have been difficult for Má's family. No doubt, Má listened to her parents espouse the vices of their South Vietnamese neighbors. Northerners were horrified at how the South Vietnamese exposed their skin to the sun instead of valuing a lighter complexion.[7] My grandparents would have done the same. Northerners complained about how the South Vietnamese were more laid back and splurged on unnecessary items.[8] My grandparents would have done the same. My grandparents would have warned Má not to allow these people to influence her behavior. Being in this society may have caused them to emphasize even more the value of hard work, how to manage money, and the importance of the business sense they had learned from their parents. Although Má never specifically told me, moving to the south must have been a culture shock that took years of adjustment. The success of Má's family in this new environment showed a dogged determination not only to live but to thrive.

Má was twenty-nine when Saigon fell to the communists. All around, South Vietnamese people desperately tried to leave the country. Since escaping this time meant moving by herself with small children to an entirely different country, Má knew it would be more difficult for her than it was for her parents. Wisely, Má stayed, relying on the camouflage of strange neighbors and poverty to protect her from the communist onslaught. Year after year, she exchanged the largest portion of her earnings for gold, which she hid in the hole under the cooking rocks. She watched and listened in the market as she sold her rice and vegetables. Her carefully worded questions sounded more like curiosity than fact gathering.

According to rumors, many people escaped successfully, while many others died due to exposure, hunger, thirst, drowning, pirate raids, and other dangers. People caught trying to escape lost everything, especially homes and property. In addition, they would be sentenced to hard labor in a prison. Má weighed the risks and waited until she had gathered enough information, found the best guide, the most successful shore from which to leave. She waited until her youngest—me-- was old enough to walk the distance to the smuggler's ship. Quietly, she discovered how to contact a guide without the neighbors or even her closest friends finding out. All this time, Má kept her secrets, the secrets that eventually made it possible for me to escape.

The first time she tried to escape, she paid for three people: herself, Chị, and me. Chị and I were young; I was about ten years old, so Chị would have been around fourteen. Má waited until I was ten so that I would be able to carry myself and withstand the stress of the trip. On the day before the guide came to take us, she found a place in the mountains near her rice paddy with natural land markers. After making certain no one had followed, she dug a deep hole in the dirt and dropped in a package wrapped heavily in plastic and tape. As soon as she had refilled the hole, she jumped up and down to pack the earth, then scattered rocks and branches over the place. Even though anyone wandering in the vicinity and noticing the disturbed earth was almost impossible, she did not take any chances.

The next night, a silent man scratched at our door, and we melted into the night, Chị nervously clinging to one of Má's hands, and me skipping excitedly along while loosely swinging her other hand. We were going to America, the land of having everything I could want.

A few days later, I arrived at the home of relatives. They were bewildered at first when I walked into their hut unannounced. Má had told no one of her plans; in fact, they had not heard from Má since she moved after my father's death. They had assumed the communist government had discovered our secret and dealt with us as they did other soldiers' families. I explained how we had followed the guide through rice paddies and around villages. After long hours of walking, running, hiding, we arrived at the shore of some water. We got onto a boat, and then, there were police. The police came out to the boat and caught all of us, about fifty people or so. They put everybody in jail, except the young children. Má gave careful, simple instructions for how to walk to the relatives' huts. After asking a few people, I found them easily enough--the home of Má's oldest brother. I met him, and my grandmother, Má's mom, for the first time.

After my initial explanation, I never heard a word spoken of Má or what she had done. They told the neighbors that a distant relative had sent me to help out for a while, and the neighbors, who had become accustomed to accepting strange stories without asking questions, nodded and went about their business, unwilling to involve themselves in anything that might draw the government's unwelcome attention.

Má and Chị showed up one day, as suddenly as I had. They were in jail for only a short period of time. Jail didn't mean a four-walled cell with a bed and sink. Jail meant forced labor in a camp. I am not exactly sure what Má and Chi did at the camp, but they had to work hard. The guards fed them and made sure they had enough water and shelter to survive, but the conditions were harsh and meant to deter further wrongdoing. Chị and Má didn't show any signs of trauma after being in jail. Of course, the government found out about Má's property; they confiscated her house and the rice fields. She had nothing after she got out.

Losing the land proved difficult for Má. The loss thrusting her into deep poverty, (She refused to spend the gold she had stashed away.), She lost a tie to her heritage along with years of hard work. Má's parents most certainly gave her the initial portion of land when she married my father. As time passed Má saved her money as her parents had taught her, and bought adjacent land to expand her income and property. Having the government take away two lifetimes of hard work-hers and her parents'-must have been hard. In keeping with her quietness, Má never spoke of how this made her feel.

Má asked her brother if we could stay until she had earned enough money to purchase another "house." He agreed. No one in this province knew about Má's escape attempt. Many people had been relocated from village to village, an attempt by the communists to relax neighborhood loyalties and cause the insecure people to turn to the government for reassurance and safety. Almost no one in Má's home village recognized her, or cared that she was living among them again.

Shortly after that, we moved to a different town by the ocean, and we made another attempt to escape around the time I was eleven. This plan wasn't successful, either. Since we had been living with another relative, we didn't have property for the government to take, but Má and Chị did hard labor a second time for trying to escape the country. Once again, I lived with relatives.

When Má and Chị were released, we moved to a town called Hai Son, and we lived there for a while. Má purchased a "house": a mud-walled shack with a straw roof and a dirt floor on a tiny square of land with a well and a hole in the back yard. By this time, Má only had enough gold for one of us to go, so she planned to send Chị.

After she put down our mat at Hai Son, arranged the cooking stones, and placed the water bucket by the door, Má once again disappeared for a few days. She returned in the night, and in the morning, I noticed that the cooking stones had been moved to a different place in the hut. Má gave me a uniform, a new toothbrush and toothpaste, and a pair of sandals for school and church. We washed our faces and brushed our teeth. I made new friends, played, and made kites and got in trouble for making kites and ate and slept much like any other eleven year old boy- except that I was living in poverty, sleeping with approximately thirty thousand dollars in gold, and papers full of deadly secrets, buried not five feet away from my head.

At this new place, Má got up well before dawn to ride her bicycle to the neighboring farmer's homes in order to purchase vegetables. She then bicycled to the market place and set up her stand so that she would be among the first vendors to attract the inevitable stream of villagers purchasing daily food. We lived there for a few months, and Má still had the dreams, had the courage to go, but this time, as mentioned previously, she planned for only one of us to go because she only had enough money to pay for one, and in the event that we got caught, she couldn't afford to lose this house that she just purchased.

Deciding to send me alone must have been the hardest decision Má had to make. She must have considered the possibility long before the smuggler showed up at the hut. She knew Chị, and she knew me, and she must have known that Chị might not be able to go through with leaving. Sending her son was a much greater sacrifice than sending her daughter. In

Vietnam, the son takes care of the parents. It's a traditional society, and as the oldest son, I pretty much had the burden of taking care of my entire family, because Chị was expected to marry and go with her husband's side. As the oldest boy, when I became a man, I would make decisions for everything.

According to tradition, if I had stayed into adulthood, I would work and give Má, since she is widowed, all the money, and she would be the head of the household. Then I would get married, and my wife and I would live with her, and when Má, deemed that we were ready to move out on our own, she would buy us a house so we could move out. When my wife and I moved out, I wouldn't give Má all of my money anymore. I would use it to take care of my own family. Of course, I would still have to take care of Má, meaning that she could move in with my wife and me if she needed to do so. An alternate possibility would be that my wife and I would continue living in the house, but Má would transfer ownership of the house to me. If there was another son younger than me, I would still be the one obligated to take care of Má. By sending me away, she was giving up her security in her old age.

In addition to sacrificing her security, she

sacrificed something else. Society in Vietnam is all about pride and saving face. If she sent me away, she would no longer have a son to brag about and show off to the neighbors. The culture worries about what people think, and they worry about status. The men are dominant over there. By sending me away, Má gave up a lot of hard-earned status in her society. She couldn't tell anyone that she had sent me to America. Even though people must have suspected what had happened to me, she probably told them that I had gone to live with relatives, or that I had just disappeared.

That explains what Má was willing to do to be successful, to put her child in a better place. When I was young, I didn't understand that. I didn't understand how selfless it was of her to let me go, especially because I am the only boy in the family. There was a lot of responsibility for me, and she was willing to give that up for me to have a better life. As I matured, I understood that more and more, but when I was young, I didn't know. The older I get, the more I see how unselfish it was of her to do what she did.

Má also taught me one of life's most important lessons: *Your mind is the most magnificent thing you have. If you choose to do it, your mind will do everything possible to make it happen.* Má decided she wanted to take my sister and me to America, and when she put her mind to it she at least partially succeeded. In order to do that she had to work every angle of the problem. She had to deceive the communists, her neighbors, and, in some cases, her closest family members into thinking she was poor, so they wouldn't steal her wealth. She had to have the self-discipline to live in poverty with a small fortune at her disposal. She had to find out how to contact a smuggler, how much she would have to pay, how to package the paperwork so it wouldn't be damaged. She had to determine the right time to act, have a back-up plan, and be willing to face the consequences if everything fell through. Má, who didn't have an education beyond the fifth grade, used her mind to accomplish her biggest goal in life: getting at least one family member out of Vietnam and into America.

Chapter 10—The Real World

Má's dreams extended to the time I would be an adult, working for what I had. In keeping with this, after graduation, I focused on finding a job. One of the first job fairs I went to was at Drury Lane in Oak Brook which is near Chicago. As I was walking through, talking to people, hoping to find a job, someone shook my shoulders from behind. He must have realized by the startled look on my face that I didn't recognize him because he introduced himself as Jim Turner, the father of my high school friend. He was now an agency manager in Carol Stream for Country Financial.

Jim said, "Hieu, this is what I'm doing (selling insurance for Country Financial). If you want to do it, I'll give you a shot."

I said, "Jim, I appreciate it, but selling, that's not for me."

So, I continued my job search and realized that employers wanted you to work a lot, which I didn't mind. They wanted you to wear nice clothes, which I didn't mind. But, they didn't want to pay you anything. For me, that was a problem.

I kept thinking about Jim's offer. So, I started looking at Country Financial again, but in and around

Havana, because that's where I grew up. I found a few agencies open in that area, so I went for some interviews. The last interview sticks out the most in my mind.

Three powerful men: the agency manager, the district director, and the regional vice president, sat at a table in the room. They were all dressed in suits and were just drilling me with questions.

I remember all I could tell them was, "Listen, I don't know anything about insurance, except that I don't want to pay for it (I didn't actually say that last part). But, I can guarantee you that if you teach me how to do this: teach me the product, teach me how to sell it. I will go out and do it."

After giving my interview a respectful amount of consideration, they told me, "No."

I could have accepted their answer with the thought, "Maybe they know something that I don't."

Instead, I took their "No," as a challenge.

That stubbornness inherited from Má, and my own struggles this far, told me that I could do this, and be successful. Right then, things were tough once again. I didn't know that life was going to get a whole lot tougher and that I was going to have to draw on every ounce of persistence embedded in my character.

I called Jim back.

I said, "Is the offer still on the table?"

He said, "Yes."

I was so excited. I got the job! As long as I passed a series of tests.

The first time I took the test, I failed part of it. I was so upset at myself that I wasn't concentrating on my driving as I left the parking lot. I pulled out in front of a car, and it hit mine. My car was still drivable, but it made a bad day worse. In spite of that, on the drive home, I decided to study more and retake the test.

Another hurdle I had to clear at the same time was Project 100. The purpose of Project 100 was to get me started on the road to success in selling insurance.

I called Lauri as soon as I found out about it. I said, "Sis, I have to come up with one hundred people I know. I don't think I know that many people. And I'm supposed to call them and see about selling them insurance."

Lauri didn't miss a beat. She said, "Well, here's what you do. You name everybody in your family, every aunt and uncle, and then you go to every swim team parent, and name them, teachers that you knew at school, people that you knew from school. Especially try to think of kids that are graduating from college because they are going to be needing insurance."

By the time I hung up the phone, I had a list of one hundred names.

I thought, "I can't believe I really know that many people." [1]

Coming up with the one hundred names was part of the evaluation process, but it didn't give me the intended boost toward success. I couldn't actually sell to those people because they weren't in my district.

The next time I went for the examination, I passed the rest of the tests. Instead of bringing relief, this presented another problem. The job was in Carol Stream. I had no place to live. Mom and Dad were not in a position to help me with the money to rent an apartment, get electricity, etc., in order to live there. So, I decided to do what I do every time I hit a wall: I asked for help from good people.

Luckily, my former college roommate was living in St. Charles, near Jim's branch of Country Financial. His name was Brandon.

I called him up. First, I said, "Brandon, good news, I got a job!"

He said, "Congratulations! Awesome!"

"But the bad news is," I said, "I have no place to live."

I paused. "Can I live with you?"

He answered right away. "Yeah, I don't see that it's a problem. I don't have a job yet, but come on up."

The thing was, he still lived at home with his parents.

After thinking about it for a minute, he said, "Let me ask my parents."

A few hours later he called me back.

He said, "We'd love to have you."

I moved to Carol Stream in July of 1998. They helped me move into their finished basement in which I had my own bedroom. In addition to giving me a place to stay, they provided food; his family made it clear that I was always welcome at all meals along with having access to anything I wanted out of the refrigerator. Brandon's mom treated me like a fourth son. She did my laundry, made sure I ate, opened her house to me in every way. His dad did the same.

Back then, in the first month working for Country, you didn't get paid. In the second month, you did. So, my first paycheck wasn't until the end of August, two months later. Although his parents wouldn't let me do much to help around the house, they did let Brandon and me mow the lawn. I felt terrible for the burden I was placing on them. When I asked for help, I only wanted enough to get me past whatever roadblock I was facing. I didn't want anyone to carry me or do it for me. Therefore, I wanted to get my own place as quickly as possible.

So, as soon as I got paid the first time, I found a small, one-bedroom apartment with a kitchen and a living room. Before I moved out, I offered to pay Brandon's parents rent for the time that I had stayed with them. I told them I would pay whatever amount they thought was fair, even if I had to pay them a little at a time. They said, "No." This wonderful family let me live with them, fed me, and didn't take any money. What a great start.

In addition to getting my own place, I needed a different vehicle. Up to this point, I had been driving the same old truck I had bought in high school, and the problem with that was: it had no air conditioning. Whenever I had to drive anyplace for my job, I usually wound up sweating from the heat. Showing up to an appointment, sweaty, in a suit, just wasn't going to get me any new clients. Since I had a steady income, Dad co-signed for a car loan. Again, I only needed the help in the form of the co-signer; the responsibility of making the payments was entirely up to me. I didn't expect Dad to help with the payments. The car I purchased had one amenity: air conditioning. Manual windows and a radio completed the "luxury" of this vehicle. It cost me a total of $11,000.

When I started, Jim was the agency manager. I worked as an agent under him. For months, every time I got a paycheck, I wanted to quit. I had a college education and could barely pay my bills. In order to get by, I ate a lot of noodles because they were inexpensive. Sometimes I skipped meals.

Jim assured me that if I stuck it out, I would see the light at the end of the tunnel. Even though I became discouraged at times, I was determined that I was going to succeed. Also, I gauged myself against the people ahead of me. They might be smarter, but I had the work ethic. I was willing to work as hard as, or harder than, they were in order to be successful

My biggest obstacle was that I didn't have a natural market. Most people have a natural market when they start: brothers, friends, friends of friends. I didn't have anyone. Facebook, LinkedIn, and other networking opportunities didn't exist. My area had a large Vietnamese-American population; however being of Vietnamese heritage didn't mean that I would automatically get Vietnamese clients. There were two reasons for this: first, as stated previously, I was new to the area; second, my Vietnamese was choppy.

Instead of quitting, instead of expecting someone to bail me out or do it for me, I decided that I wanted to be successful at this; I decided to go get it. But I realized that it might not come to me right away. It might take years of hard work and sacrifice to reach my goal.

I asked Jim's assistant to order all of the phone books in Carol Stream. I started in a cubical. All of the phone books were stacked taller than me. I called every name in the phone book: A-Adams to W-Williams. Any names I could pronounce I called.

I got so many "No's" that when I got a "Yes," I hung up anyway.

I called right back and said, "Oops! Something's wrong with the phone."

Since Angel and I hoped to get married the following summer, she moved in with me that January of 1999. She worked two jobs. One job was as a teacher's aide at an elementary school; as soon as school got out, she drove to a daycare where she worked until six p.m. With our paychecks combined, I didn't have to eat noodles anymore. However, our finances were still a struggle. Basically, we lived paycheck to paycheck. That's not what we wanted. We wanted to have a surplus so that we could save for a rainy day. We couldn't make definite plans for our wedding until I was comfortable that my job provided enough to support us. Since the man supports the family in Vietnamese culture, Má always preached to me to make sure I could take care of my family. I carried this value with me all of those years. Although Angel had a teaching degree which could supplement our income, I wanted to be the source of stability.

Once I had the leads, I started asking my customers for referrals. Then, I had two different sources of clients coming in. I would also go into business districts to introduce myself to the business owners. Even though my Vietnamese was rough, I did stop by Vietnamese restaurants and nail salons. That was scarier than cold calls because of the language barrier along with my distance from the Vietnamese culture.

Business picked up enough after Angel moved in, that we decided to plan a June wedding. When we set the date, I knew I had to spill the beans to Má. I told her during our next phone call.

I said, "Má, I'm getting married in a few

months."

After a moment of silence, she said, "To who?"

"Her name is Angel."

"That doesn't sound like a Vietnamese name."

"It's not. Angel is white."

"I forbid you to marry her," Má said adamantly. "All those American women do is get divorced. If she gets mad at you for any little thing, she'll divorce you."

"That's not true," I told her.

"Come over here," she said. "I'll find a wife for you."

"You know I can't do that," I said.

"Then find a Vietnamese-American couple with a nice daughter. Ask them to arrange a marriage for you," she told me.

I tried to keep the frustration out of my voice when I said, "If I decided to find a Vietnamese girl and marry her, it would end in divorce anyway because I don't know the culture anymore."

"You can learn the culture. Any Vietnamese girl would be lucky to have you," she insisted.

I continued. If I do that just to satisfy you, my life is going to be miserable. You have to trust me. I love Angel. I couldn't be happy with anyone else."

"I disown you," she said. I heard a click at the other end. I had expected her to argue with me; I hadn't expected her to disown me. I decided to give her some time to get used to the idea of a non-Vietnamese daughter-in-law.

Wedding, June 5, 1999
Photo courtesy of J.C. Photos

Angel and I married in June of 1999. A few weeks after the wedding, a letter came for me from

Vietnam. The handwriting was Má's.

Since I am not good at reading Vietnamese, I took it to one of my clients and asked him to read it to me. She apologized and said that, obviously, I'm right. The letter said that she didn't want me to have to go through a broken marriage. She wanted to make sure that I'm happy. A few days later, I got a phone call from her, and we were talking again like nothing had happened.

During this phone call, I shared some good news with her: Angel was pregnant. Má showed the same enthusiasm she would have if we had lived next door to her. Thinking about having another grandchild seemed to dissipate her last reservations about my marriage.

Ethan was born in early 2000. Angel's mom drove up from Havana to stay with us for a week. Consequently, she was at the apartment on Ethan's first night home. She and Angel gave Ethan his bath before putting him in his crib. I was already asleep. Their whispers must have woke me because I went to check on him in his room across the hall. When I saw him, I decided to get him out of his crib so he could sleep beside me.

I was drifting off again when the light flipped on.

"Um, Hieu, we can't find Ethan." Angel stood in the doorway with her mom peering at me over her shoulder.

"I've got him," I said, pointing to the bundle beside me.

"I'll take him back to his crib," Angel said.

"I stayed close to Má when I was little," I explained. "I want him close to us."

Despite Angel's reservations about Ethan suffocating in our bed, he slept with us for a few nights, then slept in our room in the pack-in-play for a few months.

Ethan was a fussy baby. He cried every time we got in the car and fought while we put him in the car seat. He hated sleeping in his crib. He did not want anyone to hold him except for us. I really think it was because he was only used to being around us.

A few months after Ethan was born, Angel took a job as a nanny. As part of her job, she tutored the children to keep them caught up with their school work. I was still working seven days a week. Having a baby changed our social lives in a way we didn't expect.

We started having children right away while our friends waited. This was difficult at times because we lived so far away from family and didn't have a babysitter. Our friends were still going out and invited us, but we would have to turn them down due to lack of a babysitter.

I made it to career agent, independent contractor with Country Financial, in two years. Most people take four to five years; many others don't make it that far. Perseverance, determination, hard work, and help from good people when I needed it brought me to that level of success. As soon as I reached this level, I moved into my own office. Since I was unable to afford my own secretary, I shared one with another agent.

Angel was able to finally find a teaching position, so we had a little more money coming in, which was good, because after two and a half years of marriage, we found ourselves expecting another child, this time in the fall. That year, 2002, I earned my first Agency incentive trip, destination: Hawaii. Angel's parents kept Ethan. Even though he was safe, Angel cried a lot because she missed him. Country paid for our flight, a really nice hotel, and two meals a day. At that time, Angel and I were still struggling to get by, so the cost of our lunch the first day was a shock: $50.00. After that, we decided to eat breakfast as late as we could, share an appetizer or snack in the afternoon, and then have the dinner that

Country provided.

Alex was born in the fall of 2002 when Ethan was almost three. As soon as Alex was born, Ethan was a completely different kid. He was helpful and wouldn't leave Alex's side. He didn't fight us at bedtime or fight when we put him in the car. The boys shared a bedroom, so we just had to tell Ethan to be quiet so he wouldn't wake up Alex. He took our words seriously when we said, "You have to be a good big brother and show Alex what to do."

Alex was the best baby. He did not like to be held much; he just wanted his blanket and his bed. He and Ethan were always really close. Alex fell asleep as soon as he got in the car. One time after visiting our parents, we were driving back home. Alex ate peanut butter crackers in the car just as we were leaving Havana. About twenty minutes into the three hour car ride, he started crying. It was dark so we couldn't really see him. I knew that if I ever once stopped because one of our kids was crying, I would have to stop every time, and our car rides would be miserable. I refused to pull over; I did yell at him to stop crying. When we got home, we realized he was covered in hives from the peanut butter. That is when we found out he has a peanut allergy. I felt so bad for not stopping.

By this time I had been with Country Financial for over three years; my business was successful enough that I could spend money on advertisement. I also purchased leads from Country Financial; they compiled this list of leads from people who expressed an interest in Country Financial by signing up online. I worked weeknights and weekends. Angel and I had a goal: to build my business before our kids were in school. If we could reach a certain level of financial stability, we would be able to spend time with our kids instead of working all of the time. Together, we saved toward that goal.

Although we were trying to save money, we started looking for a new home in the summer of 2003. Our current starter-home was small, and since we wanted to have a larger family, we knew it was time to move. We found the perfect house, within our budget, and moved into it in August 2003.

The next summer, Evan was born. He was also a good baby but having three small children made our lives chaos. In order to leave for work on time, we had to get the boys ready early in the morning. Most days, by the time we left, Angel and I were frustrated and at least one of the boys cried all the way to the sitter. During the day, Angel couldn't leave teaching to take care of emergencies, so I had to explain to my clients that if the phone rang and it was the day care, I had to go, which wasn't good for growing my business. Our evenings were spent in a struggle to get everyone fed, bathed, and into bed. The house didn't get cleaned, the laundry only just got done, and Angel and I were exhausted. When we realized that the cost of three kids in day care was eating up all of Angel's income, we decided something had to change, so Angel became a stay-at-home mom.

That entailed plenty of sacrifices. We didn't go out to eat as much. I worked a few more hours. However, it worked out great for all of us. As a dad, I knew my kids were taken care of, and by the time I got home, the house was clean, the dinner was cooked, and all I had to do was play with the kids for a couple of hours and go to bed. For me, that was wonderful. Angel enjoyed this arrangement, too. Spending time with the boys was important to her. She wanted time to play with them, help them learn their numbers and letters, and to see them grow. Angel also enjoyed having the time to take care of the house and cook healthy meals for us. When I got home, I played with the boys so Angel could have some time to do what she wanted to do. The best part of this was that we were working together, as a family, toward a common goal.

Evan probably had it the easiest while he was little because for the most part, he didn't have to go to a babysitter. We soon found out that he was one we always had to keep our eye on: he was a climber. Every time we turned around he was climbing on the chairs, table, etc.

After about a year of being in our new house, we decided to paint. We had a tall step ladder out. Angel would paint during the day while Alex and Evan were napping. One day, she forgot to put the ladder away before Evan woke up. He made it to the top of the ladder before we saw him. Luckily, we got to him before he fell.

We started putting the boys in sports as soon as they turned four. Ethan and Alex played tee ball. I think Evan was so tired of going to their games that he decided he didn't like baseball. We made him play one season to just try it out, but he hated it. It didn't help that he got hit across the cheek with a baseball bat when he walked into Alex's path. After that, Evan started playing soccer. Evan was always very tiny; the women thought he was so cute running up and down the field. He seemed too small to be able to keep up with the other kids, but he did and actually scored several goals each game. We began to notice that he played better on cloudy days. We asked him why and he said when it was cloudy, he wasn't able to chase his shadow!

When our oldest started kindergarten, Angel decided to babysit to supplement our income. Going back to work still wasn't practical because the little ones would need daycare. When our youngest started kindergarten, Angel was ready to go back to work, and I supported that decision. With her added income, we could save more money. With her added income, we could save more money.

After staying home for so long, she had a hard time getting back into teaching. She worked as a sub for the first two years, then worked an additional two years as a paraprofessional. A job finally opened up in the same district as the kids, which helped us because she and the kids would all have the same days off.

Ethan and Alex were able to play tee ball together one year, and I was their coach. After that year, they were on separate teams. I always had a tough decision to make when it came to whose team I was going to coach. Once Ethan turned nine and started playing travel ball, I focused more on Alex. I was able to coach Alex from the time he was seven all the way to when he was fourteen years old. Alex always had a good team and won many tournaments. I was able to coach Evan's soccer team one season, but coaching soccer just wasn't for me. So Alex was the lucky one that got dad as his coach.

Eventually, we were financially stable enough to afford to fly myself, Angel, and our three boys to Vietnam for a couple of weeks. This was in July 2010. Having the boys meet Má was important to me because I knew she would love them. I also wanted my boys to know their history first-hand. I tell them, *"Never forget where you came from: good or bad, you need to know your heritage."*

Má's misgivings about Angel also motivated me to want to take my family to see her. Má's opinion mattered to me; I wanted her to be proud of me and to have status in her community because of my accomplishments and those of my family. I wanted her to be able to speak of us in a way that would elevate her—in the minds of others as well as in her own mind.

Angel and I were not in a position to build her a new house, but we were able to send her money on a regular basis. By now, Má lived in a plywood hut with a metal roof. The updated outhouse was concrete; the user scooped water from a bucket into the hole to wash the sewage through a pipe and down a hill in the back yard. Beyond this, not much had changed. What impressed Má the most was that Angel and the boys were able to stay for two weeks at her hut. She heard that people in our culture would never be able to stay at a place like hers: no air conditioning, no running water, no bathroom—just a hole in the ground. We slept on mats at night and ate food cooked in a pot over a fire.

Má and Angel hit it off almost at once. Má kept saying that she wished that she could communicate directly with Angel in a mother and daughter type of way. Speaking directly to a person provides an intimacy that speaking through a translator cannot give. Má may have wanted to pass along advice, ask questions about Angel's life with me, or asked questions about me that only a person living with me could answer. In addition, there may have been some cultural ideas that she wanted to pass on to my wife that she couldn't say through me. Of course, for them to be able to communicate directly with each other would have been awesome. Angel and the boys, too, regretted that they couldn't personally communicate with Má.

I always jokingly said to her and to Angel, "Hey, you can communicate through me, and you will never be upset with each other because whatever you say, I can translate so you guys never get mad at each other."

My sons loved her because she was all about eating. She spoiled them. She got them all of the fresh fruits; she killed a bunch of chickens so they could eat them. They thought it was the greatest thing. She loved them, and they loved her.

Just like when I was little, she was always fanning the boys. The first time she did it, they looked at Angel and me like, "Is it alright?" We indicated that it was. After that, they grinned every time she got her fan out. One day we went on a trip which involved walking up what seemed like a million steps. On the trip down, Angel's legs kept shaking really badly. As soon as we arrived back at the hut, Má rubbed some store-bought herbal ointment on her legs. Angel was leery at first, but soon, her legs felt better. Má treated Angel just like one of us when she rubbed her arms, back, and legs in a motherly way. I was glad they were comfortable enough with each other for that to happen.

Má valued education. For my boys, her grandkids, she valued the fact that they got their education. This was once again, due to status. She wanted her grandkids to be better than the other women's grandsons.

She would say, "You gotta make sure they get through high school."

I would say, "Má, high school is not an option. High school is minimum now days."

Although she was satisfied with my answer at the time, the conversation inevitably came back to the boys' education. Over the past thirty plus years, she must have carried on almost daily conversations like this with me in her head.

The night before we left, I said, "Má, remember that conversation that we had (about my marriage)? I'm telling you, you have to trust me."

She started crying. When she regained her composure, she told me that she was happy that I had a beautiful family.

In spite of what I wanted, I was not able to bring Má to the United States. At one time, I tried to get her to come over here, to visit for a few months, just for her to see what it's like. The Vietnamese government wouldn't approve it. They wanted me to build her a brand new house so that she would have something to make her want to go back to Vietnam. Although I was able to send her money and supplies to improve her quality of life, I regret that I hadn't achieved the level of financial success at that time to be able to afford to build her a house. She applied for a passport, but the government wouldn't approve it.

Even though Má wasn't around as much as we would have liked, her ideals have a definite influence on the way we raise the boys. We always instill good manners and behavior in them. We always encourage them to do their best and to take care of each other. They have chores to do around the house, but we do not give allowances or spend huge amounts of money on their birthdays. They have what they need and always get the present they ask for at Christmas and for their birthdays. We have always talked to them about saving money and opened saving accounts for them when they were little. They are expected to put some of their birthday money in savings and are able to spend the rest. When each turns sixteen, he gets a job. We pay for their car insurance and gas money, but the rest of their spending money comes from their own pay checks.

My sons have turned into young men with the best traits of all of their grandparents. Angel and I can see a little bit of each of our parents in them. In the future, I will continue to guide my sons, encouraging them toward living the life both of my moms and dads wanted for me.

Chapter 11—Going Forward, Going Back

Around 2012, I met my soon-to-be partner, Drew. Drew was new to Country Financial. Rather than being involved in sales, Drew's job was to help agents build their businesses.

We were on a break at an all-day corporate function when Drew walked up to me and said, "I hear you are from Havana."

I shook his hand. "Yes, I am."

He said, "I spent a *month* there one night. I was there for Oktoberfest. You didn't get a beer, you got a bucket. I couldn't believe people walked around drinking beer out of buckets."

I said, "You've got the right place."

We naturally fell into a conversation about goals for my business. After only a few minutes of talking, I knew I had found another good person to help me reach my goals. Conversely, I knew I could help Drew achieve what he wanted. We decided to form a partnership. After a short time, I knew we were a good match. He was at work as early as I was; he was at work as late as I was. We were like-minded.

One characteristic Drew has that I value is honesty. In business, feelings are important, but they don't drive the business. In order to better understand each other, co-workers have to be honest with each other. As my partner, Drew has to be confident that when he speaks to me, I know he's being honest, and when I speak to him, he knows I'm being honest. We have to have courageous conversations. We can do that because in the end what he wants and what I want is the same thing. When you know that about your business partner, you have the ability to express the truth without fear. Where there is respect and trust, you can have challenging conversations because you know that you're both talking about the same end goal. Without trust, and the ability to take criticism as helpful, not harmful, you can't have those courageous conversations.

I learned the "Wait Twenty-Four Hours Concept" from Drew. Sometimes I got upset at work because I had a difference of opinion with the home office, so I would write an email. A few times, before Drew was my partner, I sent them. Needless to say, they were received with less than stellar reviews. After we started working together, Drew always said, "Don't do it (send the email). Call me first. Don't send that email right now because if you do, you will regret it." [1] I learned a lot from Drew and applied it to different parts of my life.

A few years after I started working with Drew, Má called me with bad news: she was dying of cancer. After the call, I immediately flew over to spend a week or two with her while she was in the hospital. Again, I deeply regretted that I had not reached the level of financial stability necessary to bring her to the United States. She told me that if she had it to do all over again, she would never have given me up. She had no idea the price she would pay for that decision. It made me sad to think about her missing me all of those years, about her missing her little boy growing up. When I look at my own children, I don't think I could do it, send them alone to a foreign country, even if it meant a better life. Má's strength and grit never ceased to amaze me.

I was able to fly over one more time. While I was there this second time, I made funeral arrangements because I knew I wouldn't be able to afford another trip. Since I was the oldest son, tradition placed me in charge of everything to do with the funeral. In accordance with the Vietnamese focus on status, the funeral had to be elaborate.

After Má died, my sister and her sons FaceTimed and called me with endless questions about the funeral arrangements. Some of this was due to the fact that I was paying for most of it, but mostly they called because as the oldest son, it was my duty to see that the funeral was carried out in a way honoring Má.

My sister and her sons sent pictures throughout the three-day funeral ceremony. At first, Má's body lay in a clear casket in her hut. Five folded white strips of cloth which lay on the casket represented Angel, the boys, and me. Candles on either side of burning incense sat next to the cloths. My sister and her sons wore white strips of cloth tied on their foreheads as neighbors, family, and other people visited the hut to offer prayers and condolences. On the third day, a motor vehicle with an ornately decorated wooden casket came to the hut. The clear casket was lowered into this larger one which had a painting of Jesus at the Last Supper between two Angels on its side. The motor vehicle, loaded with the double casket, drove slowly behind a band composed of a saxophone player and drummers who played sad music appropriate for such a mournful occasion. Family members carrying flowers walked ahead of and behind the motor vehicle; the entire procession made its way to the church approximately a mile away. After the funeral service, the procession walked another mile to the cemetery where Má's casket was lowered into a brick rectangle.

Later, the rectangle was enclosed in black granite matching Má's tombstone which was set at the head of the site. In keeping with the importance of status, the tombstone was approximately six feet tall and four feet wide. Composed of black granite, the front had carvings of religious symbols and candles on either side of a picture of Má. Below her picture were carved words with Má's name, the date of her birth, the date of her death, the city where she died, and her age. Above her picture was a picture of the Virgin Mary between two kneeling angels. Rising another two feet above the tombstone, a grey, granite cross completed the marker.

Since I lived so far away, Má's death took some time to sink in. My sister went through a time of terrible loneliness. Má took care of everything. My sister was lost without her. Since my sister had three boys, bringing her here was not practical. One way I tried to honor Má was to continue to care for my sister and her sons. I tried to navigate this time with my sister to make sure she was alright and to help her and her three boys make the transition to life without Má.

After a few phone calls to Vietnam without talking to Má, an emptiness started to take hold of me. It was so odd that she wasn't there. I felt a sense of satisfaction that my boys were able to spend time with her before she died. I felt a deeper sense of regret that I couldn't bring her to live with us. As the years went on, I think how nice it would have been to be able to use our now-modern technology to actually see Má as we were talking to her.

After Má's death, I was able to refocus on growing my business. When Drew came on board, we had twelve people; a few years later, we had thirty-two. As we were building, we started moving people into outside offices. Eventually, I bought my own outside office. We now have one of the finest agencies in the company. Country Financial is special to me because it's my first career, my only career. People in my generation jump from job to job or career to career. My career is a part of my life.

My conviction that what I sell helps other people is the one overriding factor that makes me successful at what I do. Country Financial insurance is about *protecting people, helping people protect their families and assets, and preparing people for the future.* Two experiences illustrate what I mean.

I never believe in selling people anything or offering people anything that I don't own. If I tell you to buy this insurance, I already have it. How am I going to tell you to buy it to protect your family if I don't have it myself? I am the best Country Financial client.

I've only been challenged by a potential client once in my career. I was talking to the man in my office, making my suggestions.

He asked me, "Do you have it (this particular insurance)?"

I said, "Yeah, I do. I wouldn't recommend it to you if I didn't. "

He said, "I want to see it (your policy)."

I said, "Here's the thing. If I show you my policy, you are going to buy one, right?"

He said, "Yeah."

I pulled my policy right up on my computer and showed it to him.

I always try to put myself in the other person's situation. If I was in your situation, would I protect my family in this way? Would I do this? If the answer is "yes," then I recommend it. If the answer is "no," I don't recommend it. I have had people call me, asking about certain insurance, and I advised against it. I would rather turn your business away than to sell you something you don't need. I feel much better about myself by doing business that way. Only offering people what I would want for myself or my family, brings a satisfaction in life that can't be traded for any amount of money. Being able to sleep at night because I feel good about what I do during the day is priceless. My values say, "I'm here for you first. Yes, I'll benefit from selling you this insurance, but I'm here because I care about you."

Another example of these values was a situation with a couple who had been my clients for ten years. The wife died suddenly. The husband knew nothing about their financial affairs. She did everything. When she died, I was there every day to help him. I told him how to take care of the bills, how to write checks; I took care of the life insurance. I helped him figure out his finances so he could pay off his house.

If my clients need something, they can call me. People notice when a salesperson is not authentic, and they notice when he is. By watching me, other Country Financial employees have said, "You know he's right. This is more than what we do for a living; this has an impact on people's futures."

Working for Country Financial has given Angel and me opportunities to travel. Including Hawaii, I have earned eleven incentive trips as of the time of this publication. Our goal is for me to get to twenty incentive trips so that I can enter into

Country's Hall of Fame. Angel's parents have been able to watch the boys for us every time we are gone. This has given the boys an opportunity to build a relationship with their grandparents as well. Before the boys started school, they were able to spend the weeks we were gone in Havana, but now Angel's mom comes to our house so that the boys can go to school and their sporting events. These trips have been good for Angel and me. We miss the boys while we are away, but it has been great for us to be able to spend time together to rekindle our marriage. It's always about the boys when we are home, but the week of the trip is just for us. Once a year, we take a nice family trip to get away from the madness and recharge the family's batteries.

I am now very successful in Country Financial. I have an office with a secretary. I have people working under me. I am in a position to expand my business as I see fit. At this point in my life, most people would think I had achieved everything the young soldier and his wife dreamed of long ago. However, their dream included one more goal, implicitly understood rather than explicitly stated: I had to give back.

Chapter 12—Full Circle

After achieving my "American Dream," I wanted to help others achieve theirs. One way I did this was to coach Alex's travel baseball team for five years, from the time he was age nine until he was fourteen.

When I first started coaching, I caught on fairly quickly that sometimes parents of kids one level below the one I coached watched my team play. Valerie was one such parent. I didn't notice her as I encouraged and instructed my team: the Cheetahs. After the game was over, she and her husband introduced themselves.

My name's Valerie, and this is my husband Greg." "Nice to meet you," I said, wondering who these people were and what they wanted.

"Our son is eight. He still plays coach pitch," Valerie went on.

"So, he might be on my team next year," I said brightly, wondering if they wanted some kind of prior reassurance that I would give their son a spot.

"Well, we just wanted to say, 'Hi,'" Valerie said.

As she and Greg walked away, I noticed a group of parents standing just a few feet from us.

"What was he like?" one man asked.

Before Valerie or Greg could say a word, a woman burst out, "OOOH, that guy is intense. I'm glad our kids are not on that team because he is crazy."

"We just want our son to have fun," Greg added. "We don't want all of this intense craziness."

"Did you see how he coaches?" the first man asked.

"Yeah," Greg said. "'Well, uh, you go here, you go over there, you go play this position.'" He said, mimicking me with his arm movements.

"This guy is so unorganized, he has no clue as to what he is doing," another parent agreed.

After cheering for their sons, their voices had naturally become louder. They must not have realized that I could hear every word they were saying.

Their estimation of me was humorous. I liked that they called me the "crazy coach." I wanted my coaching, and my team, to stand out from the others, but not for how many games they won or how seriously I viewed coaching. My goals for my team extended far beyond one particular game or season. I suspected that, even though they didn't know it, my coaching philosophy was what had caught their attention. I hoped that if their sons wound up on my team, they would change their minds about me and my coaching style.

By the following pre-season, I had completely forgotten the conversation until I saw Greg show up to try-outs with his son. I laughed inside when I thought how these people might have "that crazy coach" in charge of their son's team. After try-outs, I took a few days to consider which boys to keep and which ones to cut; then, I made "the calls."

Overall, I don't like making "the calls." The ones in which I tell parents their son is on my team are great, but the ones in which I have to tell the parents that their son did not earn a spot onto my team are hard. The disappointment, and sometimes anger, are an unpleasant part of coaching.

My first call was to Greg. We didn't get off to a stellar start.

"Who in the hell is calling me at six in the morning?" he growled into the phone.

I paused. Angel was constantly telling me that not everybody is up at six, but I sometimes forget to wait until later in the morning.

"This is Hieu Tran," I said. "I am calling to invite your son to play on my travel team."

Right away, Greg said, "Of course."

I was surprised at the excitement in his voice.

Either he forgot that I was the crazy coach, or he was so excited that his son made a team that he didn't stop to think about who I was.

That first year is always a little rocky because the boys are transitioning from rainbows and sunshine all of the time, to being expected to do their jobs. They don't get applause for every crazy thing they do because it's not cute anymore. I want them to do what they're supposed to do.[1]

Also, I don't just coach baseball; I deal with life in general. In fact, for the boys and me, it's more than baseball; it's definitely about how to live your life in a way reflecting respect: respecting yourself, respecting your teammates, respecting your opponent.[2]

The first year with me is not only a transition year for the boys but also a transition year for the parents.

After the first practice, I gathered the parents around a couple of picnic tables in a veranda near the ball fields. This was a fresh team; no return players this particular year. None of the parents knew me, and I didn't know any of them—at least directly. I anticipated some resistance.

"These are my expectations for the team," I began.

The parents actually leaned forward as if they would miss something if they didn't give me their full attention.

"First," I said, "Don't pack their bags for them. They can pack their own bags."

Some of them looked at each other as if to say, "We knew it. Crazy coach starting already."

One parent boldly raised her hand. "They're only nine. What if they forget something?"

I said, "They have to be responsible for their own equipment. If they forget, they don't get to play. They're old enough to know what they need for a game and put it in a duffle."

Next rule," I continued, "No swimming on game days."

A man spoke up. "I'm not going to tell my kid he can't go swimming. Are you nuts?"

His wife pulled on his arm. I caught a whisper about not getting their son kicked off the first day.

Valerie followed that comment by asking, "Why no swimming?"

"You're tired; you're exhausted; you're drained by the time you get out of the pool," I said, tapping the table slightly for emphasis. "How are you going to play ball after that?"

"Of course you don't want to go swimming

on the day of the game. Now it makes sense," Greg said. His face turned red when Valerie nudged him in the ribs and he realized he'd said it out loud. This was good, because it broke the growing tension.

"Next," I continued when the laughter subsided, "*The Twenty-Four Hour Rule*: If you're upset about anything, wait twenty-four hours, and then come to me. Don't go to the head guy, come to me."

"Along those same lines," I added. "Rumors are fine, but when it gets to me, I will address it: good or bad."

"Finally," I said. "During the games, give me two and a half hours. The parents are not to go into the dugout; the boys are not to leave. The parents are not to be involved in the games or practices. The boys and I are operating as a unit. *We* don't need any distractions." The parents nicknamed this separation, "The Hieu Bubble."

When a rumor of frustrations with baseball helmet orders reached me, Valerie and Greg found out that the Hieu Bubble extended to adult conflicts; adult conflict in front of the boys was unacceptable. After a parent informed me of the problem, I knew I had to have a talk with Valerie. I called her that evening.

"Hey, Valerie," I said with a friendly voice. "Would you have time to meet me at McDonald's tomorrow around six?"

Valerie didn't sound the least bit nervous. "Sure, Hieu, but why don't you just come to our house after practice?"

"We need to keep this away from the boys," I responded. "Your son is at your house. My sons, including Alex, will be at my house. We need to meet someplace else."

"Um," she said. "What's this about?"

"The helmets," I said, still keeping my voice friendly.

I found out later that Valerie hung up, looked at Greg, and said, "Oh, shit. I have to go to McDonalds."

When I saw her car pull into a parking spot, I fully expected to see Greg walk in beside her, but she came alone. After a long talk over coffee and milkshakes, we worked out the situation. After that, Valerie always came to me first if she had a problem with something concerning the team.

One of our trials by fire came at the beginning of the season; I entered the team into an elite tournament playing against teams far above their skill level. At the end of this weekend, the kids, and the parents, would decide if they really wanted to play under my coaching." For the first game, I stationed myself in my customary place next to the dug-out, sitting on a bucket, wearing flip-flops.

The other team batted first. Jon, one of my players, caught a pop-fly and threw out a kid at third base. I was surprised when they didn't score on us during that first inning. As Chet ran past me into the dugout, he said, "Did you see how I did out there, coach?"

I said, "You're out there to do a job; you don't get compliments for doing your job. You get compliments when you do something exceptional."

The kid's frown lasted the entire time our team was up to bat.

By the bottom of the fourth, the score was nine to nothing—we had the "nothing." The parents and players were becoming more and more frustrated. We had two kids on and the kid up to bat hit a pop fly to center field. Anticipating that the center fielder would fumble, as he had done many times before, I signaled for the kids on base to tag up and run for it. As luck would have it, the center fielder caught the ball, giving the team time to throw out both of our runners. The parents were furious.

"What kind of a move was that?" one parent

demanded.

"You should've had them wait. That could've been our only chance at a score," another one growled.

The parents erupted into a flurry of criticism.

They also attacked the umpire. "The umpire's calling all of the plays for the other team." "How much did the other team pay you to throw the game their way?" "You need to retire."

When I signaled time out, heading to the bleachers instead of the dug-out, the adults became quiet.

I looked at every single parent and said, "Listen, we do not play that way. This is not how our team is going to behave."

I waited until I saw nods of agreement before returning to my bucket. For the rest of the tournament, no matter how badly we were losing or how inept the umpire seemed to be, the parents didn't utter one word of criticism.

That is not to say that I agreed with every call the umpire made. At this tournament, and at other games, there were lots of times that the call didn't go our way, and I would go out on the field and get the explanation. I was level headed and tried not to be overbearing. My goal was to call the umpire's attention to it, hoping that he would do better next time.

During the last play of the game, the other team had three runners on and their best batter at the plate. He hit a grounder between second and third. Jon dove to make the play, but he couldn't get to it in time. We lost.

Jon returned to the dugout with his customary scowl. Grass stains mixed with the blood on his elbows; his uniform appeared to be permanently stained.

"Great effort!" I said, giving him a high-five.

His scowl immediately turned to a grin that lasted into the next game. His effort increased also. I was glad to see that he respected me enough to work for my approval.

After the game, I told the boys to remove their hats to shake hands as a sign of respect for the other team. I wanted them to know how to lose with dignity.

During the next game, a sports drink went whizzing past my head. One of the boys caught it.

"What was that?" I asked.

"Mom doesn't want to invade the *Hieu Bubble* ," he said with a shrug that said, *I don't understand her at all.* [3]

The players' ages were eight and nine year olds, so the maturity level of the boys was all over the place. During our second game, Dalton, who played first, looked like he was going to slug the next opponent who crossed the base.

I called time out as I made my way to first.

"What's going on?" I asked, putting my arm over his shoulder.

He immediately relaxed. "They're slaughtering us."

"Beating on them's not going to help us win the game," I told him.

He shrugged.

"Focus on catching the ball," I told him. "Don't worry about the score."

Dalton lasted one more inning. The batter hit a pop fly to center and the center-fielder dropped it. Dalton threw his hat to the ground as he kicked the base.

I signaled for a kid named Barton to follow me to first.

"Dalton, go sit on the bench," I ordered him. "Barton's going to take your place."

"But," he said. "I'm your best first-base player."

"Not with that temper," I said. "Now, go."

After the game, another stunning loss, I talked to Dalton with his parents.

"First, and most importantly," I said to them, "there's more to life than baseball; this is not the end all and be all."

I looked Dalton directly in the eyes. "You need to understand that win or lose, life goes on. How you behave defines you, not how well you play baseball."

"You mean you don't want to win?" Dalton challenged.

"Yes, we all want to win," I said. "I want to win more than anyone. But at the end of the day, it's not always about winning. Do you understand?"

He shrugged.

"Your attitude has got to change before you go back out there," I told him.

His parents didn't question me."

Dalton changed because he wanted to play and because he wanted to earn my respect.[4]

Respect all comes down to your actions. Once you show people that you are a person worthy of respect, they will respect you. To be a leader, to have the respect of others, you not only have to express it verbally, but also have to show it with your actions. People often say what they want to say, but until they show it through their actions, no one will believe it. I wanted my team to show that they deserved respect through their actions.

By the middle of the third game, a boy named Jagger asked not to bat; he struggled with hitting.

I said what I would come to say to many of the kids over the course of my coaching career, "Believe in yourself, kid."

I truly did believe in every one of these boys. There were times when they came through, and there were times when they didn't, but the underlying thought was *just believe in yourself and things will happen.*

The kids made a lot of mistakes during that tournament, just as they would continue to do. I never got down on them.

I said, "OK, you made a mistake. Now, pick yourself back up, get back out there, learn from it."

During that entire tournament, we didn't just lose; we got slaughtered. We lost our final game at night, under the lights.

I took the boys out on the field afterward. I said, "OK, you just lost. You know what that feeling is like now. You don't ever want that feeling again. We're going to win everything from here on out."

That set the precedent.

They walked off that field saying, "Never again. Never again."

As much as I wanted to win, I let the boys work through their struggles. I'm going to use pitching as an example. If a boy was struggling on the mound a little bit, instead of yankin' him right away, I would let him work through it.

I was trying to show the kid, "Hey, it's ok if you're down in the count a little bit, you can still end up on top."

Sometimes the parents thought I let them stay out there too long, but that's all part of the game.

As for coaching, my thought was, "I want to win." I don't want to lose every game, that's no fun. Through my rules and expectations, I tried to put the kids in the best possible position to win. And if we won, great, and if we didn't, we tried.

I also taught my hitters, the umpire's never going to change the strike zone because you are the batter. If you, as the batter, think the ball is outside, and the umpire calls a strike, it's a strike. Whether or not you as a batter decide to swing at it, the umpire is going to call a strike there all day. Guess what? He's not going to change for you. You're going have to make a small adjustment. If he's going to call a strike on the outside all day, you're going have to hit on the outside all day. Make adjustments as you go along. That's adapting to change.

There was one team that we faced every year in the championships. I think it was just a mental thing with the boys concerning this one team because the boys always thought the other team was going to beat us. They already pulled themselves out of the game before the game even began.

I would say to the kids and parents, "We're going to lead by example. We're going to play with heart and whatever the outcome is, it is."

We did beat that team once in a while, but not as often as we wanted to. Never in the big game. We lost to them two years in a row in the championship. Those were hard losses, but we always came back the next year and tried again.

I tried to teach my players more than baseball; I tried to teach them how to be men. Five years doesn't seem to be a long time, but I coached some of them from nine years old to fourteen years old. That's huge. That's a huge time in their lives when they are developing into young men.

Parting Thoughts

In addition to coaching baseball, I started a mentoring program at Country Financial. Being successful at my job isn't easy; it takes perseverance, dedication, and a tremendous amount of hard work. As part of my dedication to giving back to society, I invite Country reps to mentoring sessions where I work with them to reach whatever goal they set. Using my life experiences is an important part of that. When we meet, I always make it clear: *I do not have a guaranteed formula for success. I do have guidelines people can use to assist in making positive changes in their lives.*

As I continue to fulfill my journey of living the American Dream, I mentor my nephews in Vietnam so that they can achieve their dreams. As far as my immediate family, I strive to be the best possible husband to Angel while I guide my sons, encouraging them toward reaching their goals with perseverance and integrity. Helping others is a way of life for me now. I want to help as many people as possible to develop what's inside of them so that they can reach their goals before giving back to others.

(Eighth Grade Speech)

American Education: Everyone Gets a Chance

Good evening, ladies and gentlemen. Since I have been in this country, I have heard that there are many problems concerning American public education. I have heard that schools are not always getting the job done when it comes to educating students. I know I haven't been here all that long, but I don't believe all this is true.

I knew very little English when I first started school here, and I was scared. But thanks to the patient people that helped me, I can now read and write, and math is my favorite subject.

The American public school is better than a lot of critics would like to have you believe. I think that everyone has an opportunity to learn and go to college.

In Vietnam, you don't. If you do not make straight A's in school, you can't go to college. If you can't go to college, you have to serve 3 years of military duty. If your parents are considered an enemy of the government, it doesn't matter what grades you get; you still can't go to college. In Vietnam, there are very little extra-curriculars offered.

I think American schools are better because it doesn't matter what grades you get, you can still get an education. In American schools, there is a much broader curriculum. In American schools, students have more access to computers. In American schools, you don't get embarrassed by the teachers when you ask them something that you don't understand. The thing I like the most about American schools is that they don't turn their back on you. Everyone who wants to get an education can get one. Believe me, I know, it is not this way everywhere.

I would like to say "thank you" to all of the teachers that worked so hard to help me, especially Mrs. S. — and to my sister Lauri. They have spent a lot of time to help me on every subject. I'd like to thank Mr. G. for his help with this speech. I would also like to thank all of you here tonight because of your interest in our school. You make all people welcome, even those like me, who come from another country. I really appreciate that! Last, I would like to thank my parents for giving me a place to live and a chance to be a part of this school system.

Thank you family and friends for all of the support over the years! A special thank you to Catherine Hackman for helping me make this book a reality.

Notes

Chapter Four

[1] Bortell, Lauri. Personal Interview. 26, June 2017. Lauri provided some background information about Tha Huong which I wove into the narrative.

[2] Coon, Tina. Tha Huong Employee, February 198--. Personal Interview. 18, June 2018. Tina Coon provided the background information about Tha Huong which I wove into the narrative.

[3] Coon, Tina. Illinois Department of Children and Family Services Child's Summary. Tha Huong/Catholic Social Services. 1 September, 1988.

[4] Coon, Tina. Tha Huong Employee, 1988-1989. Personal Interview. 18, June 2018.

Chapter Five

[1] Coon, Tina. Illinois Department of Children and Family Services Child's Summary. Tha Huong/Catholic Social Services. 1 September, 1988.

[2] Howarth, Butch. Personal interview. 02, August 2017.

[3] Schroeder, Mike. Personal interview. 10, July 2017.

[4] Olson, David. Personal interview. 28, June 2017.

[5] Bortell, Lauri. Personal Interview. 26, June 2017.

[6] Tran, Angel. Personal Interview. 25, July 2018.

[7] Bortell, Lauri. Personal Interview. 26, June 2017.

[8] Guy, Tammy. Personal Interview. 28, July 2017.

[9] Olson, David. Personal interview. 28, June 2017.

[10] Bortell, Lauri. Personal Interview. 26, June 2017.

Chapter Six
[1] Layton, Ernie. Personal interview. 15, June 2017.

[2] Olson, David. Personal interview. 28, June 2017.

[3] Bortell, Lauri. Personal Interview. 26, June 2017.

[4] Olson, David. Personal interview. 28, June 2017.

[5] Howarth, Butch. Personal interview. 02, August 2017.

[6] Tran, Angel. Personal Interview. 25, July 2018.

[7]Stadsholt, Brenda. Personal Interview. 17,

July 2017.

Chapter Eight

[1] Fitzgerald, Frances. <u>Fire in the Lake.</u> New York: Little, Brown, and Company: 1972. 36-37.

[2] IBID., 37.

[3] "Déjà Vu (1858-1961)." *The Vietnam War: A Film by Ken Burns & Lynn Novak.* Chapter: "The Most Enlightened One." Volume: One. Episode One. Directed by: Ken Burns and Lynn Novak. A Production of Florentine Films and WETA, Washington, DC. The Vietnam Film Project, LLC., 2017.

[4] Vo, Nghia M. *The Vietnamese Boat People, 1954 and 1975-1992.* North Carolina: McFarland & Company, Inc., 2006. Page 9.

[5] Vo, Nghia M. *The Vietnamese Boat People, 1954 and 1975-1992.* North Carolina: McFarland & Company, Inc., 2006. Page 11.

[6] Vo, Nghia M. *The Vietnamese Boat People, 1954 and 1975-1992.* North Carolina: McFarland & Company, Inc., 2006. Page 12-13.

[7] Vo, Nghia M. *The Vietnamese Boat People, 1954 and 1975-1992.* North Carolina: McFarland & Company, Inc., 2006. Page 13.

[8] Vo, Nghia M. *The Vietnamese Boat People, 1954 and 1975-1992.* North Carolina: McFarland &

Company, Inc., 2006. Page 15.

[9] Vo, Nghia M. *The Vietnamese Boat People, 1954 and 1975-1992*. North Carolina: McFarland & Company, Inc., 2006. Page 15-16.

[10] Vo, Nghia M. *The Vietnamese Boat People, 1954 and 1975-1992*. North Carolina: McFarland & Company, Inc., 2006. Page 1.

[11] Vo, Nghia M. *The Vietnamese Boat People, 1954 and 1975-1992*. North Carolina: McFarland & Company, Inc., 2006. Page 1.

[12] Duplicate of Marriage Certificate: Exact Copy from the Original. No: 0051. Republic of Viet Nam; Province of Long Khanh,, District of Dinh Quan, Village of Phuong Tho. 14, June 1968. Certified: Civil Status Official: Tran Van Phu.

[13] "*Déjà Vu (1858-1961)." The Vietnam War: A Film by Ken Burns & Lynn Novak*. Chapter: "The Most Enlightened One." Volume: One. Episode One. Directed by : Ken Burns and Lynn Novak. A Production of Florentine Films and WETA, Washington, DC. The Vietnam Film Project, LLC., 2017.

[14] Vo, Nghia M. *The Vietnamese Boat People, 1954 and 1975-1992*. North Carolina: McFarland & Company, Inc., 2006. Pages 16, 17.

[15] Descriptive List and Military Service

Record of Sergeant Tran Em/R. Force/DU. Unit: Long Khanh Section, General Administration Office. Certified -3. July, 1974 by Warrant Officer Moang Trung Muc, Chief of Record Office. Translated 06 December 1988. Translator: Son Lam Hong.

[16]"Territorial Forces." Vietnam War Dictionary: Territorial Forces. VietnamGear.com. http://www.vietnamgear.com/dictionary/territorial%20forces.aspx Copyright 2005-2014. Accessed 01 July, 2018.

[17] "Vietnam Conflict Map." Hammond Incorporated. New Jersey: Hammond Incorporated, 1991.

[18] Descriptive List and Military Service Record of Sergeant Tran Em/R. Force/DU. Unit: Long Khanh Section, General Administration Office. Certified -3. July, 1974 by Warrant Officer Moang Trung Muc, Chief of Record Office. Translated 06 December 1988. Translator: Son Lam Hong.

[19] "Vietnamese New Year (Tet)." Vietnam Online. Vietnamonline.com. https://www.vietnamonline.com/tet.html . Accessed 01 July 2018.

[20] Descriptive List and Military Service Record of Sergeant Tran Em/R. Force/DU. Unit: Long Khanh Section, General Administration Office.

Certified -3. July, 1974 by Warrant Officer Moang Trung Muc, Chief of Record Office. Translated 06 December 1988. Translator: Son Lam Hong.

[21] Duplicate of Marriage Certificate: Exact Copy from the Original. No: 0051. Republic of Viet Nam; Province of Long Khanh,, District of Dinh Quan, Village of Phuong Tho. 14, June 1968.

[22] Descriptive List and Military Service Record of Sergeant Tran Em/R. Force/DU. Unit: Long Khanh Section, General Administration Office. Certified -3. July, 1974 by Warrant Officer Moang Trung Muc, Chief of Record Office. Translated 06 December 1988. Translator: Son Lam Hong.

[23]Vo, Nghia M. *The Vietnamese Boat People, 1954 and 1975-1992*. North Carolina: McFarland & Company, Inc., 2006. Page 60.

[24] "Riding the Tiger (1961-1963)." *The Vietnam War: A Film by Ken Burns & Lynn Novak*. Chapter: "The Big Story." Volume: One. Episode Two. Directed by : Ken Burns and Lynn Novak. A Production of Florentine Films and WETA, Washington, DC. The Vietnam Film Project, LLC., 2017.

[25] Part I: Military Service and Civil Status. Established by TK/Long Khanh. KBC 4552. Ratification KBC 6144, June 12, 1974, Major

Nbuyen Van Trung, Commander TT/YTTV Long
Khanh. Translated 06, December 1988. Translator:
Son Lam Hong.

[26] Descriptive List and Military Service
Record of Sergeant Tran Em/R. Force/DU. Unit:
Long Khanh Section, General Administration Office.
Certified -3. July, 1974 by Warrant Officer Moang
Trung Muc, Chief of Record Office. Translated 06
December 1988. Translator: Son Lam Hong.

[27] "Phuoc Tuy Province, South Vietnam.
February 1972. Vietnamese students at the Jungle
Warfare." The Australian War Memorial. awm.gov.
awm.gov.au/index.php/collection/C328483.
Accessed: 01, July 2018.

[28] Descriptive List and Military Service
Record of Sergeant Tran Em/R. Force/DU. Unit:
Long Khanh Section, General Administration Office.
Certified -3. July, 1974 by Warrant Officer Moang
Trung Muc, Chief of Record Office. Translated 06
December 1988. Translator: Son Lam Hong.

[29] Descriptive List and Military Service
Record of Sergeant Tran Em/R. Force/DU. Unit:
Long Khanh Section, General Administration Office.
Certified -3. July, 1974 by Warrant Officer Moang
Trung Muc, Chief of Record Office. Translated 06
December 1988. Translator: Son Lam Hong.

[30] Nguyet, Le Anh. Lieutenant Colonel. Postal Notice: Reported "Missing in Action." Long Khanh Section. 29, May 1974. Translated 06, December 1988. Translator: Son Lam Hong.

Chapter Nine

[1] Part I: Military Service and Civil Status. Established by TK/Long Khanh. KBC 4552. Ratification KBC 6144, June 12, 1974, Major Nbuyen Van Trung, Commander TT/YTTV Long Khanh. Translated 06, December 1988. Translator: Son Lam Hong.

[2] Duplicate of Marriage Certificate: Exact Copy from the Original. No: 0051. Republic of Viet Nam; Province of Long Khanh,, District of Dinh Quan, Village of Phuong Tho. 14, June 1968.

[3] Vo, Nghia M. *The Vietnamese Boat People, 1954 and 1975-1992.* North Carolina: McFarland & Company, Inc., 2006. Pages 15, 16, 32.

[4] Vo, Nghia M. *The Vietnamese Boat People, 1954 and 1975-1992.* North Carolina: McFarland & Company, Inc., 2006. Page 18.

[5] Vo, Nghia M. *The Vietnamese Boat People, 1954 and 1975-1992.* North Carolina: McFarland & Company, Inc., 2006. Page 25.

[6] Vo, Nghia M. *The Vietnamese Boat People, 1954 and 1975-1992.* North Carolina: McFarland &

Company, Inc., 2006. Pages 33 and 34.

[7] Vo, Nghia M. *The Vietnamese Boat People, 1954 and 1975-1992.* North Carolina: McFarland & Company, Inc., 2006. Page 37.

[8] Vo, Nghia M. *The Vietnamese Boat People, 1954 and 1975-1992.* North Carolina: McFarland & Company, Inc., 2006. Page 32.

Chapter Ten
[1] Bortell, Lauri. Personal Interview. 26, June 2017.

Chapter Eleven
[1] Cali, Drew. Personal Interview. 27, July 2017.

Chapter 12
[1] Summers, Valerie and Greg. Personal Interview. 27, July 2017.

[2] Unger, Cathy. Personal Interview. 15, July 2017.

[3] Summers, Valerie and Greg. Personal Interview. 27, July 2017.

[4] Unger, Cathy. Personal Interview. 15, July 2017.

[5] Summers, Valerie and Greg. Personal Interview. 27, July 2017.

Bibliography

Bortell, Lauri. Personal Interview. 26, June 2017.

Cali, Drew. Personal Interview. 27, July 2017.

"Client Service Plan: Objective/Task Statement." Illinois Department of Children and Family Services. 1, September 1988.

Coon, Tina. Illinois Department of Children and Family Services Child's Summary. Tha Huong/Catholic Social Services. 1 September, 1988.

Coon, Tina. Tha Huong Employee February 1988-1989. Personal Interview. 18, June 2018.

"Déjà Vu (1858-1961)" *The Vietnam War: A Film by Ken Burns & Lynn Novak.* Volume: One. Episode One. Directed by : Ken Burns and Lynn Novak. A Production of Florentine Films and WETA, Washington, DC. The Vietnam Film Project, LLC., 2017.

Descriptive List and Military Service Record of Sergeant Tran Em/R. Force/DU. Unit: Long Khanh Section, General Administration Office. Certified -3. July, 1974 by Warrant Officer Moang Trung Muc, Chief of Record Office. Translated 06 December 1988. Translator: Son Lam Hong.

Duplicate of Marriage Certificate: Exact Copy from the Original. No: 0051. Republic of Viet Nam; Province of Long Khanh,, District of Dinh Quan, Village of Phuong Tho. 14, June 1968. Certified: Civil Status Official: Tran Van Phu.

Fitzgerald, Frances. *Fire in the Lake: The Vietnamese and the Americans in Vietnam.* New York: Back Bay Books, 1972.

Guy, Tammy. Personal Interview. 28, July 2017.

Howarth, Butch. Personal interview. 02, August 2017.

Layton, Ernie. Personal interview. 15, June 2017.

Nguyet, Le Anh. Lieutenant Colonel. *Postal Notice: Reported "Missing in Action."* Long Khanh Section. 29, May 1974. Translated 06, December 1988. Translator: Son Lam Hong.

Olson, David. Personal interview. 28, June 2017.

Part I: Military Service and Civil Status. Established by TK/Long Khanh. KBC 4552. Ratification KBC 6144, June 12, 1974, Major Nbuyen Van Trung, Commander TT/YTTV Long Khanh. Translated 06, December 1988. Translator: Son Lam Hong.

"Phuoc Tuy Province, South Vietnam." February 1972. Vietnamese students at the Jungle Warfare." The Australian War Memorial. *awm.gov.* awm.gov.au/index.php/collection/C328483. Accessed: 01, July 2018.

"Refugee Act of 1980." *National Archives Foundation.* www.archivesfoundation.org/documents/refugee-act-1980/. Accessed: 19, June 2018. National Archives Foundation."

"Riding the Tiger (1961-1963)" *The Vietnam War: A Film by Ken Burns & Lynn Novak.* Volume: One. Episode Two. Directed by : Ken Burns and Lynn Novak. A Production of Florentine Films and WETA, Washington, DC. The Vietnam Film Project, LLC., 2017.

Stadsholt, Brenda. Personal Interview. 17, July 2017.

Summers, Valerie and Greg. Personal Interview. 27, July 2017.

Tran, Angel. Personal Interview. 17, July 2018.

Tran, Hieu. "American Education: Everyone Gets a Chance." Speech Delivered: May 30, 1990.

"Territorial Forces." Vietnam War Dictionary: Territorial Forces. *VietnamGear.com.* http://www.vietnamgear.com/dictionary/territorial%20forces.aspx Copyright 2005-2014. Accessed 01 July, 2018. Information used by written permission.

Truong, Lt. Gen. Ngo Quang. "Territorial Forces." *Indochina Monographs.* U.S. Army Center of Military History, Waashington, D.C. First Printing: 1981. https://www.vietnam.ttu.edu/star/images/1127/11270 103001a.pdf. First Accessed: 28, June 2018.

Unger, Cathy. Personal Interview. 15, July 2017.

"Vietnam Conflict Map." Hammond Incorporated. New Jersey: Hammond Incorporated, 1991.

"Vietnamese New Year (Tet)." Vietnam Online. Vietnamonline.com. https://www.vietnamonline.com/tet.html . Accessed 01 July 2018.

Vo, Nghia M. *The Vietnamese Boat People, 1954 and 1975-1992.* North Carolina: McFarland & Company, Inc., 2006.

Made in the USA
Coppell, TX
03 December 2019

12264550R00122